GOOD
ALWAYS
WINS

GOOD
ALWAYS
WINS

Thru Tragedy, Thru Evil, Thru All Eternity

Ed Strauss

VALUEBOOKS
An Imprint of Barbour Publishing, Inc.

Published by Value Books, an imprint of Barbour Publishing, Inc., P.O.
Box 719, Uhrichsville, Ohio 44683, www.barbourbooks.com

*Our mission is to publish and distribute inspirational products offering
exceptional value and biblical encouragement to the masses.*

 Member of the
Evangelical Christian
Publishers Association

Printed in the United States of America.

Contents

Introduction

The world around us can be very beautiful at times, but it is also filled with pain, grief, and injustice. Even if we're personally safe and comfortable, we know that hardship in one form or another is a reality for hundreds of millions of people around the globe. And though we don't always know the full scope of suffering in the world, what we do know raises a troubling question: "How could a God of love allow so much evil and misery?"

Many people, when they think of suffering, picture children living in unsanitary conditions in makeshift shelters, without clean drinking water, without hope of an education, struggling to survive without basic necessities in a drought-stricken land or in impoverished circumstances. The facts are grim: Nearly 870 million people on earth today suffer from chronic malnourishment, and 15 million children die of starvation every year.

And then there are wars—from border disputes between nations, to civil wars, to ethnic conflicts, to governments locked in ongoing battles with suicide bombers and terrorists—that bring death, destruction, and displacement to countless people every year.

But we don't have to look overseas to find examples of people in pain. All around us are those suffering from cancer, multiple sclerosis, heart disease, or the aftereffects of a serious traffic accident or workplace injury. Children born with chemical imbalances or birth defects live with a measure of suffering every day. Parents who must cope with the death of a child can find the pain at times almost unbearable.

Many more people endure emotional anguish, from betrayal by a close friend or a spouse. Divorce leaves people in so much pain that they can almost feel as if they're dying. Others may suffer from anxiety and depression because of long-term unemployment, bankruptcy, or the daily stress of limited finances and rising prices.

Where is God when all this is happening?

What good can come from all this anguish?

These are urgent questions, and at times there seems to be no satisfying answers—and yet, if there truly is a God, there *must* be answers. Still, we can be baffled by the seemingly senseless violence or misery. We long to understand not only the pain of the world, but our own suffering as well, and to see God's hand and His love through it all.

That is the purpose of this book—to examine these troubling issues and perplexing questions, and to show how God indeed redeems tragic situations and brings good out of evil. A word of caution: We won't end up with simple answers, but they'll be *real* answers that make sense on a deep level.

1

Why Does God Allow Suffering?

The world is overflowing with suffering, and we and our loved ones experience grief and pain as well. Because God has given us reasoning minds and commands us to have tender hearts of compassion, we're compelled, like Job of old, to ask searching questions: "How could a God of love cause all this suffering? Or, if He doesn't cause it, why does He allow it?"

The Bible says that "God is love" (1 John 4:8 KJV) and that He is all-powerful: " 'Behold, You have made the heavens and the earth by Your great power and outstretched arm. There is nothing too hard for You' " (Jeremiah 32:17 NKJV). Yet, many would say that these statements can't both be true.

God may be all-powerful, they reason, because He created the entire universe; but like an absentee watchmaker, He then left the world to run on its own, while He stands at a distance from mankind's woes and no longer interacts with us, because He simply isn't concerned. This viewpoint is called Deism.

Either that, or they assume, like Rabbi Harold Kushner (who wrote *When Bad Things Happen to Good People*) that God cares, but He isn't quite all-powerful and can't answer all our prayers, so we shouldn't blame Him.

A third explanation is that God has given us freewill, and mankind often chooses to follow selfish instincts and to do evil, hurtful things. God has resolved not to interfere with our choices *at this time*, but at the end of time He will judge all people for the good or evil they've done.

The fourth position is that all suffering is the result of a holy God judging sin. Every volcanic eruption or earthquake or epidemic happens because God is judging a community of people for their iniquities. When an individual gets sick or is injured, or suffers financial setbacks, it's a judgment on that person's sin.

The fifth position is that all the disasters, diseases, and suffering in the world are caused, not by God, but by the devil and his demons— and are therefore intrinsically evil, something to be rejected and prayed against. At the end of time, God will punish these evil spirits, but in the meantime, they cause havoc and much suffering in the world.

So which of the above views is correct? Actually, there's a measure of truth in all of them, but any one position by itself is simplistic and gives us an incomplete understanding of the issues. We must take into account that the Bible declares that the Lord is a God of love and compassion, and that He's all-wise and seeks to bring about good in our lives.

Let's examine the first position—that God is all-powerful, but that, having created us, He then left us to struggle alone because He's not interested, or He has far too many worlds to care for to be hands-on in the affairs of one insignificant planet. Now, God *is* Lord of all Creation, and He created some 170,000,000,000 galaxies in the universe, with each galaxy containing 10,000,000 to 100,000,000,000 stars. And God Himself is bigger than the whole universe. "Will God really dwell on earth? The heavens, even the highest heaven, cannot contain you" (1 Kings 8:27 NIV).

Despite the immensity of God and His universe, He hasn't abandoned us. The Psalms state: "The LORD is good to *all*, and His tender mercies are over *all* His works" (Psalm 145:9

NKJV, emphasis added). We're His creation, the work of His hands, and He made each of us for a purpose. He didn't bring us into existence only to abandon us. Yes, God has the entire universe to take care of, but Jesus assured us that our heavenly Father knows when even one sparrow falls to the ground—and He values us much more than the birds (Matthew 10:29–31).

If you find the vastness of God mind-boggling, in contrast to His knowledge of minute details, remember that this is precisely why we worship Him as God.

The passage above says, "His tender mercies are over *all* His works." Sometimes, however, it may appear as if His tender mercies are *not* over us, and that the Lord is *not* bringing good into our lives, at least nothing we can recognize as good. It can stretch our faith to believe that when God seems distant, and we repeatedly cry out with tears—and hear nothing in reply, and see no change in our circumstances—He's actually close at hand, concerned, and feels our pain.

Now, God is always present. The Bible tells us, "The Lord is close to the brokenhearted" (Psalm 34:18 NIV). However, if a *person* gave us the silent treatment the way God sometimes seems to, we'd get the impression that he or she didn't care and was ignoring us. We'd be tempted to ignore that person in return. This is, in fact, how we often react to God.

But here's a very important point: God set up the world with certain constant physical laws. For example, having created gravity, He doesn't need to continually intervene to make objects fall to earth; having placed the world in orbit around the sun, He doesn't need to repeatedly adjust the laws of nature to make it continue to orbit. Having set the moon in motion around the earth, He doesn't continually perform miracles to make the tides rise and fall. They happen because He ordained it long ago.

This may tend to make God appear to be an absentee watchmaker, however. So how can we believe that His "tender mercies" are over us, in light of the fact that we or those around us often experience suffering? God has intervened at key points in history, and performs miracles today as well, but these are the exception rather than the rule. If miracles were the rule, we wouldn't be able to count on any of the laws of physics. But we *can* depend on natural laws. That's what makes a miracle unique. Plus, when God *does* intervene, He usually (not always, but often) does so within the context of natural laws, and makes His presence known in small, almost imperceptible, ways.

For the most part, however, God permits events in the natural world to unfold and run their course. And yet He has a benevolent purpose in all things and is determined to redeem any evil and suffering that happens. Make no mistake: Not all that happens to us in this life is good, but God is able to bring good out of it in the end. "And we know that all things work together for good to those who love God, to those who are the called according to His purpose" (Romans 8:28 NKJV).

As for the second position—that God cares immensely, but He isn't quite all-powerful—this isn't an either/or situation, as we've already noted. God can be all-powerful and caring at the same time. And He *is* all-powerful. There's nothing too difficult for Him. He says, "'I am the LORD, the God of all mankind. Is anything too hard for me?'" (Jeremiah 32:27 NIV). The answer is no. The God who created the entire universe can do anything.

This, of course, prompts the question: "If

God can quickly and powerfully act to resolve problems or suffering, *why doesn't He*?"

When I read *When Bad Things Happen to Good People*, I found I disagreed with Rabbi Kushner on several key points. For one, in an attempt to explain that suffering isn't God's fault, he takes the position that God *can't* answer prayers and prevent misfortune. Also, Kushner ignores the many verses that declare that God blesses obedience and judges sin. Yet I agree with Kushner when he says, "He [God] is limited in what He can do by laws of nature and by. . . human moral freedom."[1] God *can* override the laws of nature, but has chosen not to constantly intervene.

This is a point with which many Christians agree. Although God *is* all-powerful, He has given mankind freewill, and we often choose to follow our selfish instincts. God has resolved not to interfere with our freewill at the present time, but one day will judge all people for all the good or evil they've done. This brings us to the third possible explanation—that a great deal of suffering is caused by the exercise of our freewill.

---

1. Rabbi Harold S. Kushner, *When Bad Things Happen to Good People*; New York: Avon Books, 1983, 134.

This explanation has a good scriptural foundation, and explains why there are robberies, oppression, murders, and genocides. Mankind's inhumanity to fellow humans is a major cause of suffering in the world today. God will eventually bring them to judgment, however. He says, "'I will punish the world for its evil, and the wicked for their iniquity'" (Isaiah 13:11 NKJV). The wicked cause great suffering, and God is *not* okay with that. The Bible tells us, "God is angry with the wicked every day" (Psalm 7:11 KJV).

Human folly and selfishness also go a long ways toward explaining why millions of people in the world die of starvation. It's not that there isn't enough food to feed everyone. There is. But regional wars disrupt agriculture, and government mismanagement causes millions of children to go to sleep hungry. And people in wealthy nations thoughtlessly throw away tons of uneaten food every day. The figures are shocking: Every year, fully *one-third* of all food produced in the world—some 1,300,000,000 tons—is wasted instead of eaten!

However, the misuse of our freewill doesn't explain disasters such as earthquakes, volcanic eruptions, and tsunamis—nor does it explain why plagues and epidemics cause the death of millions. I discuss these matters in chapters 3 and 4.

———

There's another reason why God doesn't manifest all His power, and that is because He often only exercises His power in response to prayer. This verse was fulfilled in Jesus: "'A bruised reed he will not break, and a smoldering wick he will not snuff out, till he has brought justice through to victory'" (Matthew 12:20 NIV). God doesn't interfere with the laws of nature even to keep a sparrow from falling, or to break an already half-broken reed—until He finally acts to transform all nature in the fullness of time. In the meantime, however, He *does* act in response to prayer.

The obvious conclusion, then, is that we must pray. As James says in the New Testament, "You do not have because you do not ask" (James 4:2 NKJV). You might ask, however, "What about people in desperate situations who pray repeatedly, but whose prayers seem to go unanswered?" There are a number of reasons why God sometimes doesn't answer prayers immediately, but often it's because most people don't pray—or don't *persist* in prayer. The Bible says, "Be patient in trouble, and *keep on* praying" (Romans 12:12 NLT, emphasis added). Why would people *not* pray when God is waiting and willing to act? Often they lack faith that God is even listening. Yet we're called to pray fervently and persistently.

———

Let's look at the fourth position: that all suffering is a result of a holy, angry God judging sin. When you read the scriptures, it's clear that God frequently promised to punish willful sin, and that when people in the Bible continually disobeyed, He brought afflictions and troubles on them to discipline them. It's particularly clear that God promised to bless or judge His covenant people, the nation of Israel, according to whether they obeyed or disobeyed His laws. The clearest example of this is found in Deuteronomy 28. (Although we won't detail that here, it's well worth reading and found in Appendix A beginning on page 129.)

God warned that He'd bring suffering on His people if they sinned against Him, and this is where we get the idea that God judges people for their sin. However, this kind of direct intervention was usually reserved for His covenant people. God expressly said, "'You only have I chosen of all the families of the earth; therefore I will punish you for all your sins'" (Amos 3:2 NIV). As for other nations, "'In the past he permitted all the nations to go their own ways'" (Acts 14:16 NLT). Though God sometimes intervened to judge pagans, He didn't necessarily do so on a continual basis. When He did punish them, it was primarily because they had oppressed His people or directly opposed Him. Examples of this are Egypt, Aram, Assyria, and Babylon.

God also chastises His people today, those who have faith in His Son, Jesus Christ. But don't forget that God has loving purposes for this: "Those whom I love I rebuke and discipline. So be earnest and repent" (Revelation 3:19 NIV). Scripture admits that this process can be difficult: "No discipline seems pleasant at the time, but painful. Later on, however, it produces a harvest of righteousness and peace for those who have been trained by it" (Hebrews 12:11 NIV).

But let's be clear: This discipline generally refers to temporary suffering, from which, after a while, we're relieved. The discipline (however serious or painful) passes, we learn our lessons, and the suffering comes to an end. Or, in the case of a handicap or a medical condition, it teaches us patience, trust, and humility; and though it may not be fully removed, we learn to live with it, to manage its symptoms, and in return gain deep life lessons we wouldn't have learned otherwise.

But is it logical to take this principal—that God chastises the disobedient—and apply it as a blanket explanation for *all* human suffering, no matter how severe? Is this actually what the Bible teaches? No, it's not. We examine this further in the next chapter.

———

Finally, there's a fifth explanation: that disasters, disease, and suffering happen when Satan afflicts people. Suffering can therefore be blamed on the devil and plainly declared to be evil and a curse, "the works of the devil" (1 John 3:8 NKJV).

This is why a large part of Jesus' ministry on earth went to alleviate the suffering that Satan caused: "'God anointed Jesus of Nazareth with the Holy Spirit and with power, who went about doing good and healing all who were oppressed by the devil'" (Acts 10:38 NKJV). Jesus gave a clear contrast between His purposes and the devil's purposes: " 'The thief comes only to steal and kill and destroy; I have come that they may have life, and have it to the full' " (John 10:10 NIV). "For this purpose the Son of God was manifested, that He might destroy the works of the devil" (1 John 3:8 NKJV).

But how can Satan cause so much trouble if God is in charge of the world? Well, even though the Bible declares that the earth belongs to God (Psalm 89:11), it also says, "The earth he has given to mankind" (Psalm 115:16 NIV). God intended for mankind to " 'have dominion over the. . .earth' " (Genesis 1:28 NKJV), but when Adam and Eve fell, the devil gained behind-the-scenes control. That's why Jesus repeatedly called Satan " 'the ruler of this world' " (John 14:30 NKJV) and Paul referred to him as "the god of this world" (2 Corinthians 4:4 KJV). (See also Luke 4:5–6.)

This, therefore, is one of the main reasons there's so much evil and suffering on earth. Satan and his demons are limited beings, but they can cause suffering on a vast scale. Demons incited the Nazis to kill Jews in Auschwitz and Treblinka and other death camps. And the killing fields of Cambodia and ethnic cleansings in Bosnia and

Rwanda were definitely the "works of the devil." Demons, like the evil people they incite, exercise freewill and cause untold amounts of suffering— and God will ultimately punish them for it.

———

Although humans are the physical agents who inflict suffering on other humans, the examples of evil above are of such a massive scale that it's clear that larger, darker spiritual forces are at work. Bart Ehrman is highly critical of faith in God; nevertheless, he accurately says in his 2008 book, *God's Problem*: "The evil people do to one another can be so massive, so wicked, so overwhelming that it is hard to imagine it as simply people doing bad things. . . . Evil is sometimes so far beyond palpable that it is demonic."[1]

However, when it comes to believers who love and trust God, the devil can only directly attack them if God gives permission, as we see from Job's example (see Job 1–2):

"Satan replied to the LORD, 'Skin for skin! A man will give up everything he has to save his life. But reach out and take away his health, and he will surely curse you to your face!'

---

1. Bart D. Ehrman, *God's Problem: How the Bible Fails to Answer Our Most Important Question—Why We Suffer* (New York: HarperCollins, 2008), 258.

"'All right, do with him as you please,' the LORD said to Satan. 'But spare his life.' So Satan left the LORD's presence, and he struck Job with terrible boils from head to foot" (Job 2:4–7 NLT).

According to this view, if people have a relationship with God, He puts a barrier around them that the devil can't get through. Satan complained that God had "'made a hedge around [Job], around his household, and around all that he has'" (Job 1:10 NKJV). When people sin, however, this creates gaps in the wall, allowing Satan to gain entry and cause misery. The devil is called "the accuser of our brothers and sisters, who accuses them before our God day and night" (Revelation 12:10 NIV). The evil one accuses believers and demands the right to afflict them.

Sometimes, Satan makes the case—as he did with Job—that a person *will* sin if tested enough. After Peter insisted he was willing to go to prison and to die with Jesus, Jesus told him, "'Satan has asked for you, that he may sift you as wheat. But I have prayed for you, that your faith should not fail'" (Luke 22:31–32 NKJV).

One reason God *allows* such testing is because it gets rid of the chaff and purifies believers. This was true not only for Job and Peter, but for many other believers as well. Job recognized that God was ultimately the one allowing all his troubles, and said, "'When He has tested me, I shall come forth as gold'" (Job 23:10 NKJV).

———

Whatever your views on the *cause* of suffering, a great number of people suffer in our world every day—and, for the most part, God does not intervene. We ask why He didn't prevent the 2004 Indian Ocean tsunami from killing more than 230,000 people. Why He doesn't intervene to keep 15 million children from dying of starvation every year, or prevent an additional 2 million from perishing for lack of clean drinking water and sanitary living conditions.

You may begin to wonder whether we're any nearer a definitive answer to the question, "Why does God allow suffering?" Not if you're looking for a simple, one-size-fits-all answer. That's because we can't pluck a single verse from scripture and hold it up as *the* answer. When it comes to human suffering, there's *not* one simple answer. A complete answer has many facets.

Bear in mind that, comparatively speaking, we're also working with grade-school addition, wondering why things don't add up, while God works with advanced mathematical formulas. Many things we're unaware of must be factored in.

"'For My thoughts are not your thoughts, nor are your ways My ways,' says the LORD. 'For as the heavens are higher than the earth, so are My ways higher than your ways, and My thoughts than your thoughts'" (Isaiah 55:8–9 NKJV).

2

What Does the Bible Say about Suffering?

As Christians, we claim that the Bible has the answers to all of life's questions. This is a logical conclusion if God is indeed real and the Bible is His inspired Word. Therefore, we reasonably expect that the scriptures will also answer one of life's most difficult questions: "How can a God of love allow all the misery and suffering in the world?" But if this answer is there, it appears to be hidden quite well.

The Bible addresses the issue of suffering in some detail, and very early in human history. The foundation of our understanding is found primarily in Job, a lengthy book devoted entirely to the subject of suffering and pain, which serves as a key for understanding suffering in the rest of scripture.

You may have heard the view that the book of Job is a piece of historical fiction written during the days of King Solomon, when much wisdom literature was penned—or even later. But there's strong evidence that it describes real events and was written in the Patriarchal Era, at the end of the Middle Bronze Age, the very period in which it claims to be set. This makes it, after Genesis, the earliest scripture that God gave to the Hebrews.

The book of Job is set in the ancient land of Uz, which was near Edom and Midian. Uz still existed in Jeremiah's day, and the prophet makes reference to it in Lamentations 4:21. Back in Job's day, however, the Israelites were slaves in Egypt and experiencing great suffering. "The Egyptians made the children of Israel serve with rigor. And they made their lives bitter with hard bondage—in mortar, in brick, and in all manner of service in the field. . . . Then the children of Israel groaned because of the bondage, and they cried out; and their cry came up to God" (Exodus 1:13–14; 2:23 NKJV).

Moses, attempting to help a fellow Israelite, killed an Egyptian taskmaster and had to flee to Midian. He lived there in exile for the next forty years, until he had an encounter with God at Mount Sinai. There God told him, "'I have surely seen the oppression of My people who are in Egypt, and have heard their cry because of their taskmasters, for I know their sorrow'" (Exodus

3:7 NKJV). God then sent Moses to Egypt to deliver His people.

Most people never wonder how the Israelites got the book of Job and how a story about a pious Arab ended up included among the Hebrew scriptures—but the answer is obvious: Job was written in Uz about 1600 BC, when the Israelites were slaves in Egypt, and Moses read a copy of it while he was next door to Uz, in Midian. Job's story no doubt resonated with Moses while he was languishing in exile, and it surely would have spoken to the Israelites in their suffering. So Moses brought it with him when he returned to Egypt in 1445 BC. In fact, Moses was probably the one who wrote the introduction and conclusion to the book of Job we have in our Bibles.

The Israelites made their exodus from Egypt, and a year later were at the foot of Mount Sinai, where God gave the Law to Moses (Numbers 9:1). While Israel was at Sinai, God made a covenant with them, promising to bless and prosper them if they obeyed, and to cause suffering if they disobeyed (Exodus 34:10; Deuteronomy 28). However, the Israelites received the Law *after* they had read the book of Job, and the Law didn't supersede it. The Law, with its specific covenant promises, was superimposed on the foundation established by Job, which explained why God allowed suffering. The Law supplemented but did not displace the book of Job.

———

When we look at Job's story, we see that he lost all his wealth and his sons and daughters in one day—convincing him that this was no coincidence, but that God Himself had sent this disaster (Job 1:13–21). Then Job was stricken with painful, disgusting sores—and suffered for *months* before his friends arrived (Job 7:3–5). Day after day, he thought intensely about his suffering. But it made no sense to him, because, like his friends, Job had been taught to believe that God always rewarded righteousness and judged sin. Yet he could think of nothing he had done that warranted such punishment.

Nevertheless, even though Job had lived his life in a bubble of prosperity and favor, he had secretly wondered why suffering *didn't always* follow neat rules. Why, for example, were multitudes of the innocent killed by plagues, along with the guilty (Job 9:22–24)? It comes to light that Job had harbored a growing fear for years—that even though he did his best to live righteously, it might not be enough to keep away all suffering (Job 3:25). And indeed it hadn't.

At first, Job's friend Eliphaz told him to persevere, that because he *was* righteous, God would eventually restore his fortunes (Job 4:3–7). Another friend, Bildad, agreed: "If you are pure and upright, even now he will rouse himself on your behalf and restore you to your prosperous state. . . . He will yet fill your mouth with laughter" (Job 8:6, 21 NIV). But Job had already worked his way past that backup doctrine. After months of intense suffering, he was no longer convinced that God was obligated to bless him financially and personally, even if he remained faithful (Job 6:11). This issue caused him such mental distress that he wished to die (Job 6:8).

Finally, a third friend, Zophar, had heard enough. He was convinced that, because no man was completely righteous, Job must be guilty of secret sins—in fact, God wasn't even judging him as much as he deserved (Job 11:6). Zophar urged Job to repent, and promised that his fortunes would be restored if he did (Job 11:13–20). From then on, the book is filled with Job's continuing protests of innocence, and his three friends' insistence that he must be guilty.

The doctrine that God always blesses obedience and judges sin existed before the Law of Moses was delivered, and Job's friends were convinced he was suffering because he had broken God's laws. They argued from every possible angle that God always judges wickedness—and even though they couldn't *think* of any sin Job had committed, they were convinced that he *must* have sinned. Why? Because he was suffering (see Job 4:7–8; 11:6, 10–15, 13–17; 15:1–6).

One after another, they lectured Job and tried to try to get him to confess that he was suffering because God was judging him. Finally, a frustrated Eliphaz let loose a vehement tirade, accusing Job of a whole litany of sins—perhaps hoping that if he hurled enough accusations his way, something would stick (Job 22:5–11).

Yes, we do sin and God does judge sin, but when all is said and done, the entire point of the book of Job is to show that simple cause and effect *did not* apply in his case—and by extrapolation, it doesn't apply to *much* human suffering. Why would we have the book of Job in the Bible if its lessons applied to Job and to no one else? Disobedience is a reason for suffering, but it's not the only reason. Sometimes the righteous suffer hardship through no fault of their own. Why does God allow this? Often, it's because He's working out a plan.

As we know, God blessed Job after his prolonged suffering (Job 42:10–17). In the New Testament, James reminds us: "Brothers and sisters, as an example of patience in the face of suffering, take the prophets who spoke in the name of the Lord. As you know, we count as blessed those who have persevered. You have heard of Job's perseverance and have seen what the Lord finally brought about. The Lord is full of compassion and mercy" (James 5:10–11 NIV).

When we're in the midst of suffering, it can be extremely difficult to picture God as "full of compassion and mercy." Yet it's not easy for God to see us suffer. He permits it, but only reluctantly. "Though He causes grief, yet He will show compassion according to the multitude of His mercies. For He does not afflict willingly, nor grieve the children of men" (Lamentations 3:32–33 NKJV).

———

We see this same theme of suffering in the book of Ruth, written some 650 years after Job. In the days of the Judges, there was a long famine in Israel, so Naomi, her husband, and their two sons were forced to sell their land for what they could get for it; then, when that money ran out, they uprooted and emigrated from Bethlehem to Moab to find food. The sons married Moabite women; but just when it seemed they had found a little relief and happiness, tragedy struck again: Naomi's husband and both sons died.

Pause for a moment and put yourself in Naomi's position. Imagine how you'd feel. She was overwhelmed with grief and financially destitute. Yet what had she done wrong? Thoroughly beaten down, unable to make any further sense of her life, she decided to return to Israel. As she was saying good-bye to her former daughters-in-law, she lamented, "'Things are far more bitter for me than for you, because the LORD himself has raised his fist against me'" (Ruth 1:13 NLT).

Naomi returned to Bethlehem, and her old neighbors were overjoyed to see her again, exclaiming, "Isn't this Naomi?" You can hear the depths of Naomi's suffering in her answer: "'Don't call me Naomi [which means *pleasant*],' she told them. 'Call me Mara [which means *bitter*] because the Almighty has made my life very bitter. I went away full, but the LORD has brought me back empty. Why call me Naomi? The LORD has afflicted me; the Almighty has brought misfortune upon me'" (Ruth 1:20–21 NIV). Naomi had suffered like Jacob before her, who lamented after years of misfortune, " 'Everything is against me!' " (Genesis 42:36 NIV).

But we know the end of Naomi's story: Her daughter-in-law, Ruth, had returned with her to Israel, married a wealthy landowner, and gave birth to a son—who, as a later writer was careful to point out, became the ancestor of David, Israel's greatest king. Naomi was once again happy and secure. So was her suffering merely to punish her for sin? No. Naomi knew she wasn't deserving of such punishment, which was why she was confused, depressed, and bitter. She was like a female Job. Yet through it all, God was working out His purposes.

Job also became bitter when he suffered, because he knew he hadn't committed any sin that warranted such severe punishment. He took pains to list all the good things he'd habitually done (Job 29:11–17), and even called down curses upon himself if he'd done anything unjust (Job 31:5–35). His suffering made no sense. At some point, however, a later writer (likely Moses) revealed that Satan had moved God to test Job. So, he had his explanation in the end. And Naomi understood the reason for her misery in the end as well. When we meet God, we, too, shall finally understand the reasons for our suffering. But we may not understand at all before then.

The Bible makes it very clear that all trouble is *not* a result of God's judging of sin. If it were, the most wicked would be quickly and severely punished. Yet, this was what caused Job to question: "'Why do the wicked live and become old, yes, become mighty in power? . . . Their houses are safe from fear, neither is the rod of God upon them. . . . They spend their days in wealth'" (Job 21:7, 9, 13 NKJV).

As a psalm writer named Asaph observed, God *doesn't always* judge the wicked for their sins immediately; instead, they often continue to prosper and live trouble-free lives:

"I was envious of the boastful, when I saw the prosperity of the wicked. For there are no pangs in their death, but their strength is firm. They are not in trouble as other men, nor are they plagued like other men. Therefore pride serves as their necklace; violence covers them like a garment. Their eyes bulge with abundance; they have more than heart could wish. They scoff and speak wickedly concerning oppression; they speak loftily. . . . Behold, these are the ungodly, who are always at ease; they increase in riches" (Psalm 73:3–8, 12 NKJV).

———

But, as Asaph realized, the wicked *would* get their just dues in the end. "When I thought how to understand this, it was too painful for me—until I went into the sanctuary of God; then I understood their end. Surely You set them in slippery places; You cast them down to destruction. Oh, how they are brought to desolation, as in a moment!" (Psalm 73:16–19 NKJV).

Despite the covenant promises the Israelites had been given, they were forced to come to terms with the disparity of the wicked prospering and having a life of ease while sincere believers struggled to make ends meet. They realized that, although material prosperity was desirable, and abundance certainly preferable to adversity and lack, it was better to be poor and righteous than wicked and rich. David writes, "Better the little that the righteous have than the wealth of many wicked" (Psalm 37:16 NIV).

By New Testament times, the concept of "the pious poor" was firmly established in the Jewish psyche. Jesus Himself expounded on this, saying: "'Blessed are you poor, for yours is the kingdom of God. Blessed are you who hunger now, for you shall be filled. Blessed are you who weep now, for you shall laugh. . . . But woe to you who are rich, for you have received your consolation. Woe to you who are full, for you shall hunger. Woe to you who laugh now, for you shall mourn and weep'" (Luke 6:20–21, 24–25 NKJV).

Jesus underscored this teaching by telling a story: "'There was a certain rich man who was clothed in purple and fine linen and fared sumptuously every day. But there was a certain beggar named Lazarus, full of sores, who was laid at his gate, desiring to be fed with the crumbs which fell from the rich man's table. Moreover the dogs came and licked his sores'" (Luke 16:19–21 NKJV).

Jesus did *not* say that the rich man was rich because God had blessed him; nor that he was clothed in elegant attire and enjoyed daily banquets because he claimed the abundant life; nor that he enjoyed good health because he was righteous. Jesus also did *not* say that Lazarus was forced to beg because he had a poverty mentality, nor that he was diseased because God was judging him for sin; nor that having dogs lick his festering sores was a sign that God had abandoned him. Rather, this story echoes the suffering of Job in the Old Testament. Lazarus is the Job of the New Testament. He epitomizes the suffering poor.

Jesus finished this story by saying that Lazarus died and was carried by angels to Abraham's bosom. The rich man also died but went to Hades. When he cried out, "'Father Abraham, have mercy on me. . .for I am tormented in this flame,'" Abraham replied, "'Son, remember that in your lifetime you received your good things, and likewise Lazarus evil things; but now he is comforted and you are tormented'" (Luke 16:24–25 NKJV).

You may be receiving "evil things" right now. Like Job or Naomi or Lazarus, you may be suffering, and you may not be able to understand why God allows it. But one day, Jesus promised, you *shall* be comforted. And you *will* understand. "Now we see things imperfectly. . .but then we will see everything with perfect clarity. All that I know now is partial and incomplete, but then I will know everything completely" (1 Corinthians 13:12 NLT).

———

The Bible doesn't fully explain why individual suffering occurs, but it shows us the attitude we should have toward those who are in pain. After Job's friends accused him of sinning and bringing disaster upon himself, he responded, "'I have heard many things like these. . . . I also could speak like you, if you were in my place; I could make fine speeches against you and shake my head at you. But my mouth would encourage you; comfort from my lips would bring you relief'" (Job 16:2, 4–5 NIV).

Jesus encouraged, comforted, and brought relief to the distressed. "When he saw the crowds, he had compassion on them, because they were harassed and helpless, like sheep without a shepherd" (Matthew 9:36 NIV). Thus, an Old Testament prophecy was fulfilled in Jesus' life: "'The Spirit of the Lord God is upon Me, because the Lord has anointed Me. . . . He has sent Me to heal the brokenhearted. . .to comfort all who mourn'" (Isaiah 61:1–2 NKJV).

We are to do the same. Paul advises us to

be moved with compassion for one another. He tells us, "Weep with them that weep" (Romans 12:15 KJV). It's difficult to weep with someone, however, if we harbor suspicion that he or she is suffering for sin against God. If we entertain the idea that God Himself is angry and is standing back to let the person "stew in their own juices," we feel justified in doing the same.

Why are some believers so quick to pass judgment on others? Because there *are* examples of the truly wicked in the Bible, and God speaks firmly about their suffering judgment. Thus, when distress and anguish come to people around us, it's very tempting to assume the worst—like Job's friends. It's easy to conclude that the person must have sinned. And, in some cases, it might be true. We simply don't know. But, even as God allows others to go through suffering, He's also closely watching *our* reaction to see what's in our hearts—whether we'll sit back and judge, or reach out with mercy.

3

Why Disease and Disabilities?

When we or a loved one are stricken with diseases such as cancer or a norovirus, or suffer from debilitating medical conditions such as cerebral palsy, Alzheimer's, or lupus, we might assume that God is punishing us for some sin. Even if we aren't inclined to think that way ourselves, well-meaning friends may ask if we've given thought to any sin in our lives that may have brought this grief upon us. Job told such people, " 'What miserable comforters you are!' " (Job 16:2 NLT). He added, " 'If only you could be silent! That's the wisest thing you could do' " (Job 13:5 NLT).

Even unbelievers sometimes have more sympathy than Christians. At least they don't usually hint that people brought such suffering upon themselves. They may not be moved with compassion to help, but at least they don't pretend to be *trying* to help. Often when they hear the results of your medical report, they say, "That's too bad. I really feel for you." It's not much, but when you're already suffering, you appreciate that someone isn't trying to pile guilt on top of your suffering.

On the other hand, some of the most compassionate and nonjudgmental people you could ever meet are Christians. You see them interacting gently with the mentally ill, caring lovingly for those with Down syndrome, and selflessly working to alleviate the suffering of cancer ward patients. They may be medical missionaries, homecare workers, or just the person sitting next to you in church, but they reflect the character of Christ, and you can see the love of God in their faces. What is their secret?

Like Paul, they can say, "Christ's love compels us" (2 Corinthians 5:14 NIV). And somehow you get the impression that they're less caught up with guessing someone's secret sins, and are more concerned with alleviating suffering and letting Christ love others through them.

This is not to say that sin isn't a serious matter, or that it doesn't cause sicknesses, mental problems, psychosomatic illnesses, or compel us to engage in self-destructive lifestyles, or weaken our immune system making us more susceptible to disease. It does all these things. Nor is it to say that God doesn't ever judge sin by sending sickness to individuals. He does. If you read the Bible, you'll see that at times God either allowed the disobedient to get sick, or, in certain cases, sent a disease upon them (see Psalm 107:17; 2 Chronicles 26:16–21; Acts 12:20–23).

But does that mean diseases and accidents are *always* the result of sin? Is it a hard and fast rule? The answer is a definite "no."

Let's consider something else: The Gospels are clear that disease is often caused by Satan and his demons. In the course of healing a person, Jesus frequently cast out an evil spirit that had caused the sickness (see Matthew 9:32–33; 17:14–18). However, this wasn't always the case. Most of the time, when healing someone, Jesus simply exercised His power (see Matthew 9:1–8, 18–30; 20:29–34; Luke 13:11–16). Most people weren't possessed by an evil spirit, even if one had *caused* them to become sick. Thus, Jesus "went about doing good and healing all who were oppressed by the devil" (Acts 10:38 NKJV).

But again, many people conclude that God wouldn't have *allowed* the devil to afflict people in the first place unless they had sinned. They quote this passage: "Like a fluttering sparrow or a darting swallow, an undeserved curse does not come to rest" (Proverbs 26:2 NIV). They insist that if you're "cursed" with sickness, you must have done *something* wrong. But this is the same line of reasoning that drove Job's friends to accuse him. Besides, this passage is about vindictive people cursing others, and its point is that curses won't alight on the innocent. The New Living Translation states: "An undeserved curse will not land on its intended victim."

The Gospel of John tells us: "Now as Jesus passed by, He saw a man who was blind from birth. And His disciples asked Him, saying, 'Rabbi, who sinned, this man or his parents, that he was born blind?' " (John 9:1–2 NKJV).

The disciples' question about whether the man himself had sinned, causing him to be born blind, doesn't mean they believed in reincarnation—that he must have sinned in a past life. Rather, so many rabbis were fixated on the thought that *all* disease was punishment for sin, that if a baby was born with a medical condition or disability, either God had judged the child to punish his parents for their sins, or *the fetus* had sinned before birth, bringing judgment down upon himself!

They probably tortured this interpretation out of the psalm where King David laments, "Behold, I was brought forth in iniquity, and in sin my mother conceived me" (Psalm 51:5 NKJV). Of course, if David had sinned before birth, why wasn't *he* born blind or handicapped? (Actually, the point of this verse is actually that all humans are born with a sinful nature.)

Jesus' disciples asked the question, "'Rabbi, who sinned, this man or his parents, that he was born blind?'" And Jesus answered, "'Neither this man nor his parents sinned, but that the works of God should be revealed in him'" (John 9:2–3 NKJV). Jesus then healed the man, and this work of God caused many people to believe in Him (John 10:41–42).

The "works of God" are not only healing—although it's wonderful when they are! Sometimes God does a work in our lives and uses sickness or infirmity to accomplish it. As one believer confessed, "Before I was afflicted I went astray, but now I keep Your word" (Psalm 119:67 NKJV). He adds, "My suffering was good for me, for it taught me to pay attention to your decrees" (Psalm 119:71 NLT). Suffering also causes us to pray and draw closer to God; and it moves us to acts of compassion and self-sacrifice.

As painful as our experiences can be, God knows that good can come from them. He told the Jews: "'I have refined you, but not as silver is refined. Rather, I have refined you in the furnace of suffering'" (Isaiah 48:10 NLT). In biblical times, silver was melted in a furnace, at which point the dross (impurities) rose to the surface and was scooped off. In the same way, when we pass through the furnace of suffering, it has the potential to purify us. It can also bring out virtues; for example, "suffering produces perseverance" (Romans 5:3 NIV).

Suffering can, if we allow it, accomplish good. After Joseph's brothers had mistreated him and sold him as a slave into Egypt, he told them: "'You meant evil against me; but God meant it for good, in order to bring it about as it is this day, to save many people alive'" (Genesis 50:20 NKJV). However, it can take years for God to work out His plan. He doesn't immediately intervene every time we're suffering injustice or pain. Joseph had to endure thirteen years in slavery and in prison before God brought the intended good out of his experiences. In many cases, we may not know until we get to heaven the full reasons why we, or a child, were afflicted with a medical condition or fatal disease.

What about healing for our bodies in the here and now? There is ample scriptural evidence that God can and does heal people supernaturally—both in the Old and New Testaments. Much of Jesus' public ministry was dedicated to healing people—and the apostle James gives us detailed instructions on how to pray for healing (James 5:14–15). But there's somewhat less evidence that it is absolutely God's will to heal *everyone* who is sick, if only they have faith.

While it's often true we don't receive answers because we lack faith, the fact is, God has not promised to *always* heal. Paul, who had outstanding healing gifts, couldn't heal a faithful coworker, Trophimus, but left him sick at Miletus (2 Timothy 4:20). Timothy had "frequent illnesses" of the stomach. Unable to heal him, Paul gave him practical health advice (1 Timothy 5:23 NIV). Paul himself had a "thorn in the flesh" that he couldn't get rid of, despite praying repeatedly about it (2 Corinthians 12:7 KJV).

———

When a stranger is sick, the question of why can be academic. But when that someone is *us*, the question becomes intensely personal. Or when our own child or the child of a loved one becomes sick, it causes us to ask, "Why *him*, God? Why *her*? What did this innocent child ever do to deserve this?" We wonder what possible good such affliction can accomplish in a child. And if there's no apparent purpose, but it's "just something going around," then why didn't God prevent the child from contracting it?

We now know that germs (bacteria and viruses) are responsible, and that an inactive lifestyle and poor diet are often catalysts for illnesses. But while we can and should take responsibility for our *own* dietary/exercise choices, the question comes up: Why did God create viruses and bacteria in the first place?

This is a valid question. After all, plagues have caused great suffering and death. Some twenty-five million died of the Justinian Plague in the Eastern Roman Empire from 541–542. The bubonic plague claimed one hundred million lives in Europe and Asia from 1338–1351. More recently, seventy-five million died worldwide from influenza (a flu pandemic) from 1918–1920. And from 1981–present, more than twenty-five million have died from the HIV/AIDS pandemic.

Bacteria cause diseases from strep throat to leprosy to the bubonic plague, so many people think that *all* bacteria are pathogens. But most are harmless and multitudes of bacteria do tremendous good in the world. They're essential in recycling nutrients, and other living creatures couldn't survive without them. Some five hundred species of bacteria live in the human body. There are ten times more bacteria inside us than actual human cells, and many of these bacteria produce vitamins or help us digest food—especially starches—and absorb nutrients. They're an integral part of God's plan.

Why then do some bacteria cause disease and death? It wasn't this way when the world was first created, when "God saw everything that He had made, and indeed it was very good" (Genesis 1:31 NKJV). The present reality, however, gives evidence that we live in a corrupted, fallen world. Mankind's disobedience brought a curse upon the earth (Genesis 3:17–18; Isaiah 24:5–6), and this was when certain bacteria mutated and became malignant.

Viruses, for their part, cause sicknesses such as influenza, hepatitis C, dengue fever, and HIV. They're simple entities incapable of even self-replicating; they must invade other cells (whether bacteria or plants or humans) and commandeer them to produce more viruses. Since they can't even reproduce without hosts—and since they cause much evil and almost zero good—they probably weren't part of the original creation. Very likely, they came into being at the Fall, morphing from existing bacteria or plasmids (pieces of DNA that can move between cells).

Even evolutionary scientists theorize that this is how viruses came about, though they don't believe in the Fall of mankind and the corruption of creation. But God told Adam, " 'The ground is cursed because of you' " (Genesis 3:17 NLT). Paul added, "For the creation was subjected to frustration. . .by the will of the one who subjected it [God]," and that one day, when the kingdom of God is established, "the creation itself will be liberated from its bondage to decay." In the meantime, "the whole creation has been groaning as in the pains of childbirth right up to the present time" (Romans 8:20–22 NIV).

Until the day that creation is renewed, there are practical, loving things that we can do to alleviate suffering—and as Christians, we *should* do if we possibly can. After all, some two hundred million people in the world have malaria, and it kills more than seven hundred thousand people a year. Yet, if recognized early, malaria infections can be completely cured. And there are effective medicines for those who already have the disease. But in many cases they can't afford the medicine.

Cholera is caused by unclean water and poor sewage disposal; nearly five million people get sick from cholera every year, and of those, 120,000 die. This is precisely the reason that Christian aid organizations focus on digging wells for impoverished communities, and send healthcare workers to teach villagers about proper sanitation. We can be part of the solution by donating to such organizations.

———

Speaking of the earth being in the pangs of childbirth, we often ponder this beautiful passage of scripture when a baby is born. David exclaimed to God: "You made all the delicate, inner parts of my body and knit me together in my mother's womb. Thank you for making me so wonderfully complex! Your workmanship is marvelous—how well I know it. You watched me as I was being formed in utter seclusion, as I was woven together in the dark of the womb. You saw me before I was born" (Psalm 139:13–16 NLT).

But do we *still* think that birth is a wonderful miracle when a child is born blind or imperfectly formed in some way? They, too, were designed by God. As He asked Moses, " 'Who makes the mute, the deaf, the seeing, or the blind? Have not I, the LORD?' " (Exodus 4:11 NKJV). Do we still say, "Your workmanship is marvelous," or do we wonder whether the child was cursed—like the Yanomami tribe of the Amazon, which has such superstitious fears of anything different (even twins are considered a birth defect) that they bury them alive or abandon them in the jungle to die?

We do well to remember the love that some beautiful Christians have as they patiently care for an elderly parent; or the special needs teacher who encourages a blind child to learn Braille and to be all she can be. Good also wins when we travel to developing nations to bring medical services to neglected people groups; when we compassionately care for lepers; when we descend into the slums of Calcutta to love and care for the sick and the dying.

Yes, this attitude can be taken to an extreme,

when people count poverty and misery as a blessing and glorify it—but compassion is a tremendous motivating force for good, causing Christians to reach out to alleviate suffering. It's what causes us to stop on the Jericho road to help an injured man from a despised ethnic group (Luke 10:25–37). As Jesus said, "'Truly I tell you, whatever you did for one of the least of these brothers and sisters of mine, you did for me'" (Matthew 25:40 NIV).

Love truly is God's answer to the problem of suffering in the world. This doesn't mean, however, that we shouldn't wrestle with the problems of what *causes* suffering. Christians have long been in the forefront of discovering cures for disease, and medical scientists must constantly ask questions as they seek cures. They must ask, "What caused this?" when seeking to contain a pandemic. There is also nothing wrong with asking why God allows suffering. We *should* be moved by suffering, and we *should* ask questions and seek answers.

———

Here's a question: "If God designs everyone from birth, and the blueprint for an entire human being is in our DNA, why does God give people DNA that causes them to be born with medical conditions?" Well, God *gave* humanity good DNA originally, but our genetic codes have become damaged. When the code is altered and becomes "unreadable," and this faulty DNA replicates, it causes cancerous cells or transmits incomplete or imprecise genetic information to the next generation—resulting in defects and illnesses.

It's a well-known fact that ultraviolet radiation from the sun is a leading cause of damage to our DNA. Fortunately, both the ozone layer and Earth's electromagnetic field block much of this harmful radiation. (The ozone layer absorbs about 98 percent of the sun's medium-frequency UV light.) In addition, God made our cells good—very good—at repairing damage. It takes a lot of radiation to alter our DNA. Plus, scientists believe that Earth's magnetic field was three times stronger in the past. There were a lot of good things working in our favor after the Creation.

Many Christians also believe that a water shield in the form of ice crystals surrounded the earth before the Flood. When this fell as rain (Genesis 7:11–12) and the magnetic field weakened, the damage in our DNA began to accumulate at faster rates. Some scientists mock the idea that a layer of ice crystals once surrounded our planet. Yet they barely bat an eye when you remind them that Venus, the world next door, has an upper atmosphere of sulfuric acid 10–15 miles thick—or that a planet named 55 Cancri E, discovered in 2011, appears to be composed largely of diamonds.

In addition, God designed our nerves to feel pain. He knew there'd be pain in the world, and wanted to be sure we felt it. While this may seem to epitomize an unloving God, pain is necessary. What if you felt *no* pain when you put your hand on a stove? You'd be badly burned. As it is, you jerk your hand away, thanks to your pain sensors. Dr. Paul Brand, an award-winning physician known for his groundbreaking studies on leprosy, thoroughly examines this issue in his 1997 book *The Gift of Pain*.

After God created the world and humans, He declared everything "very good" (Genesis 1:31). Not just good, but *very* good. That was God's original plan. Did He know that humanity would sin and fall? Yes, He did. Did He realize this would bring suffering upon the human race? Yes, He did. But His long-range plan was to bring an end to all suffering and to make things right again.

God didn't originally intend suffering, disease, and death, but in His ongoing victory of good over evil, He continually redeems calamities and brings good *out of* suffering. "And we know that all things work together for good to those who love God, to those who are the called according to His purpose" (Romans 8:28 NKJV). This doesn't mean that all things that happen are, in themselves, good. Some are very painful. What it *does* mean is that God is able to take even our illnesses and suffering and cause them to work out for a good purpose in the end.

One of those purposes is that, when we have compassion on those suffering around us, we do acts of mercy to help them. This fulfills God's command to love our neighbor as we love ourselves. It fulfills Christ's law. "Carry each other's burdens, and in this way you will fulfill the law of Christ" (Galatians 6:2 NIV). The Bible says, "You have fed them with the bread of tears, and given them tears to drink in great measure" (Psalm 80:5 NKJV), but it also says, "Weep with them that weep" (Romans 12:15 KJV).

Best of all, the Bible says, " 'Blessed are you who weep now, for you shall laugh' " (Luke 6:21 NKJV). "Because thou shalt forget thy misery, and remember it as waters that pass away" (Job 11:16 KJV). One day, " 'God will wipe away every tear from their eyes; there shall be no more death, nor sorrow, nor crying. There shall be no more pain' " (Revelation 21:4 NKJV). So we must keep this life's sufferings in context: This life is not the end. There is heaven hereafter, and "our light and momentary troubles are achieving for us an eternal glory that far outweighs them all" (2 Corinthians 4:17 NIV).

Our present physical bodies may be weak, suffering from disease, or handicapped—but one day they'll be transformed into powerful, eternal bodies. "Our earthly bodies are planted in the ground when we die, but they will be raised to live forever. Our bodies are buried in brokenness, but they will be raised in glory. They are buried in weakness, but they will be raised in strength. They are buried as natural human bodies, but they will be raised as spiritual bodies" (1 Corinthians 15:42–44 NLT). This beautiful promise holds true both for us and for our loved ones.

Yes, life is often unfair—grossly unfair. And we're not just talking about the death of thousands in a cholera epidemic in an impoverished land, or a loved one dying slowly of cancer in an affluent nation. All things aren't made right in this life. They can't be. But they will be made right in the next. This hope has been tremendously comforting to millions of people down through the ages, and for good reason.

4

Why Natural Disasters?

═══════════

When earthquakes, volcanoes, and tsunamis wreak havoc, they're called "acts of God." This is a legal term used by insurance companies to refer to circumstances beyond human control; but many people believe that these *are* specific acts of God—that is, that these aren't *natural disasters* at all, but are actually supernatural interventions in the physical world by God, who personally causes the destruction.

This viewpoint is often born of two motivations: First, people sincerely desire to give glory to God, and according to their understanding, for Him to be all-powerful, rule the nations, and be active in the world today, He must constantly intervene in all matters both great and small. They fear they're denying God's omnipotence and glory if they don't say He's responsible for everything that happens. Second, on a personal level, such a view offers assurance that things aren't out of control. The righteous aren't stricken along with the guilty by mere chance.

According to this line of thinking, God has good reasons for causing disasters. But what could His reasons be? If an earthquake strikes China and kills several thousand people, they speculate that God judged them for not believing in Him. If an earthquake strikes Italy, they suggest that God judged them because they're not true Christians. If an earthquake strikes the United States, they assume God is judging our nation for turning away from the truth. If an earthquake strikes their own neighborhood, however, they don't know what to think. Perhaps their neighbors sinned?

Such explanations don't take into consideration that the overwhelming majority of earthquakes are too small to cause any damage or even be noticed; they're so inconsequential that they can be detected only by delicate seismological instruments. What could be the purpose of those smaller temblors? Does God simply enjoy spending His time, day in and day out, causing microscopic tremors in the earth? Or does the devil cause earthquakes? That's even *less* likely, because he's a finite being, far less powerful than God. So is there another explanation?

A scientific explanation has to do with plate

tectonics. Seismologists have determined that the earth's outer layer (the lithosphere) is broken up into seven or eight large plates, and these plates are slowly moving, driven by the spreading ocean floor and large convection currents in the earth's mantle. Where plates collide, mountain ranges such as the Himalayas are thrust up. Where one plate slides under another, mountains are built through volcanic activity (the islands of Japan and the Andes Mountains are examples of this). The enormous pressures from the sliding and colliding plates are released in bursts of energy called earthquakes. If earthquakes happen at sea, they can cause tsunamis, also known as tidal waves. In addition, most of the earth's volcanoes exist in the Ring of Fire on the edges of the Pacific Plate, and along other plate boundaries. Earthquakes and volcanic eruptions are natural by-products of Earth's composition, not caused by God's continual intervention.

Of course, God is perfectly capable of *making* earthquakes happen. He had His people settle in Canaan right beside the Arabian tectonic plate (the cause of the Jordan Rift Valley), so they have experienced plenty of earthquakes throughout their history. Some of these earthquakes were huge and destructive, like the one described in Amos 1:1. Another may have caused a landslide, creating a dam upriver and drying up the Jordan so the Israelites could cross (Psalm 114:3–7). Others were just big enough to draw people's attention to important events—such as the earthquake that occurred when Jesus died, or the earthquake when He was resurrected (Matthew 27:50–54; 28:1–2).

The question this raises, however, is not whether moving tectonic plates can cause such incredible damage and loss of life, but rather, why didn't God create the earth *without* them? "God. . . fashioned and made the earth, he founded it; he did not create it to be empty, but formed it to be inhabited" (Isaiah 45:18 NIV). Since He formed it to be inhabited, why didn't He make it a less dangerous place for humans while He was at it?

Well, to make Earth habitable, it had to have three things, besides water and oxygen: (1) enough gravity to hold the atmosphere in place; (2) a magnetic field to shield us from the sun's UV rays and cosmic radiation; and (3) rapid rotation to give us night and day and prevent temperature extremes. Earth meets all these requirements. Its mass not only creates gravity, but it also causes intense pressure and heat. At its very center, Earth's core is hotter than the surface of the sun. Heat radiates out from this solid core, and together with the rapid rotation of the planet, causes convection currents in the fluid outer core above it. This is turn generates electric currents that creates the earth's magnetic field.

All of these are good, absolutely necessary things. But a by-product of these forces is the earth's mantle, just above the molten outer core. Heat escaping from the mantle causes hot convection currents to circulate slowly. These cycles cause the crust above to break into tectonic plates and move, which causes earthquakes, volcanoes, and tsunamis. It's part of having a habitable planet, and God will not constantly intervene to neutralize these natural effects.

———

In many countries with semi-active volcanoes, people build their homes and farm the land near the volcanic cones because there are few other places to live. They enjoy the benefits of rich soil, but they may also have to quickly evacuate. Those trade-offs come with the territory (see Ecclesiastes 10:9). The danger is when people refuse to leave, like those who ignored the warnings to flee Mount St. Helens in 1980, and who died in the cataclysm. As Christians, we sometimes push the envelope by telling ourselves that God loves us, so He will protect us anyway and prevent disaster from striking.

Even Jesus, however, refused to presume on God's intervention. During His temptation in the wilderness, "the devil took Him up into the holy city, set Him on the pinnacle of the temple, and said to Him, 'If You are the Son of God, throw Yourself down. For it is written: "He shall give His angels charge over you," and, "In their hands they shall bear you up, lest you dash your foot against a stone."' Jesus said to him, 'It is written again, "You shall not tempt the Lord your God"'" (Matthew 4:5–7 NKJV).

When Christians who live on the East Coast of the United States hear that a destructive hurricane is about to make landfall, they often pray for God to turn away the storm. And sometimes God does a miracle and causes the storm to veer back out to sea. But it's best to prepare, even while praying to be spared. And if the order is given to evacuate, it's wise to comply.

Those who live on the West Coast are often

advised to prepare for earthquakes. There are simple things a person can do, which can alleviate needless additional suffering. Even if all that happens is that the power goes out for a couple of days, they'll be glad to have water and flashlights. And if they do need medical supplies and emergency foodstuffs, they'll be glad for those, too. "A prudent person foresees danger and takes precautions. The simpleton goes blindly on and suffers the consequences" (Proverbs 22:3 NLT). God expects us to do our part.

This is not to say that God can't do a miracle and protect us. He can—sometimes by keeping us from the disaster area. My brother booked a vacation in Phuket, Thailand for December 2004. At the last minute, he changed plans and canceled. If he hadn't done so, he would have been there on December 26 when the most destructive tsunami in recorded history swept ashore with a wave nearly one hundred feet high. It killed more than 230,000 people in fourteen countries, and an estimated 8,212 people died in Thailand, with some 8,457 more injured.

My brother was extremely thankful that he wasn't there at the time, but I've never heard him say that this serendipitous turn of events was due to any personal merit of his.

The Bible promises in numerous places that God will protect sincere believers. Psalm 91 is often called the "Protection Psalm," and here's part of it: "If you say, 'The LORD is my refuge,' and you make the Most High your dwelling, no harm will overtake you, no disaster will come near your tent. For he will command his angels concerning you to guard you in all your ways. . . . 'Because he loves me,' says the LORD, 'I will rescue him; I will protect him, for he acknowledges my name. He will call on me, and I will answer him; I will be with him in trouble, I will deliver him'" (Psalm 91:9–11, 14–15 NIV; see also Psalm 121:1–7).

In chapter 1, we saw that God placed a hedge of protection around Job—and it's commonly believed that Job's constant prayers and devotion were what allowed God to maintain that hedge. But the question we need to ask is this: Why was a wall of protection *necessary* in the first place? This presupposes that misfortune and accidents happen on a continual basis—whether due to the devil's attacks or caused by random natural forces—and God must put something in place to protect us from them.

You'll frequently hear testimonies of how God

miraculously protected Christians or their loved ones in the midst of danger, often due to their prayers. Prayer definitely makes a difference— not simply one desperate prayer in an emergency, but a lifelong habit of communing with God. But while we find stories of miraculous protection inspiring, in the shadow of such testimonies are the lives that *weren't* spared—and many of these, too, were sincere believers. How do we account for this? How do we explain it?

If you know someone who was the victim of such a tragedy, this can raise painful questions: "Why was *my* loved one killed when the person right beside her was spared? Was my loved one not worthy? Was she not praying enough?" Thankfully, people who survive disasters are usually grateful and have the humility not to say that the reason *they* were spared was because they loved God more, or that they were special. They're aware that "there, but for the grace of God, go I."

Many times, those who escape harm experience survivor's guilt. They, too, ask, "Why was I spared when others equally worthy were taken?" For the survivors, as well as for those grieving their lost loved ones, there are often no easy answers. Sometimes it seems that the best survivors can hope for is that they will live each day as a gift, and that those who mourn can hope that time will heal and that they will eventually gain, if not always a completely clear perspective, then at least a measure of peace.

———

Droughts and famines are other issues that cause people to question the goodness of God—especially when children suffer and starve. Many times in the Old Testament, God is specifically described as the one who brings disaster—whether drought, earthquake, locust swarm, or plague. God warns, " 'When a land sins against Me by persistent unfaithfulness, I will stretch out My hand against it; I will cut off its supply of bread, [and] send famine on it' " (Ezekiel 14:13 NKJV).

Furthermore, the Lord says He will bring a famine to an end or stop a locust swarm, if His people repent. " 'When I shut up heaven and there is no rain, or command the locusts to devour the land, or send pestilence among My people, if My people who are called by My name will humble themselves, and pray and seek My face, and turn from their wicked ways, then I will hear from heaven, and will forgive their sin and heal their land'" (2 Chronicles 7:13–14 NKJV). This is where people get the idea that *all* droughts and famines are caused by sin.

Now, when God set up the world to be inhabited, He created it with rich soil and adequate rainfall—that is, in "the habitable part of his earth" (Proverbs 8:31 KJV). Paul said, "'The living God, who made the heavens and the earth. . .has shown kindness by giving you rain from heaven and crops in their seasons; he provides you with plenty of food and fills your hearts with joy'" (Acts 14:15–17 NIV).

God shows His love to all people, but He chose one nation to whom He frequently manifested His presence and His power. He told Israel, "'I am making a covenant with you. Before all your people I will do wonders never before done in any nation in all the world'" (Exodus 34:10 NIV). He was even actively involved with the *weather* of their land, "'a land of hills and valleys, which drinks water from the rain of heaven, a land for which the LORD your God cares; the eyes of the LORD your God are always on it, from the beginning of the year to the very end of the year'" (Deuteronomy 11:11–12 NKJV; see also

Psalm 65:9–10).

Note that some of the earth's worst droughts are mentioned simply as historical facts with no indication of their being caused by God's judgments. "And there was a famine in the land: and Abram went down into Egypt to sojourn there; for the famine was grievous in the land" (Genesis 12:10 KJV). "And there was a famine in the land, beside the first famine that was in the days of Abraham. And Isaac went unto. . .the Philistines" (Genesis 26:1 KJV).

Scientists tell us that these "grievous famines" were part of a larger global drying trend after the Ice Age. During the Middle Bronze Age, entire regions of Egypt, the Fertile Crescent, and the Indus Valley, once filled with thriving civilizations, were abandoned. This desertification also forced the Amorites out of the Syrian steppes into Mesopotamia and Canaan. Later, when Joseph was in Egypt, and a great famine was coming, God warned Pharaoh and had Joseph prepare (Genesis 41:47–49, 53–54). Though the Bible tells us that God sent that drought, there's no indication it was a punishment for sin, and it, too, was part of the changing global weather pattern at that time.

There are different weather patterns in the world today, and while some of us enjoy gentle winters, balmy springs, and mild summers, the weather is not so gentle in other regions and nations. Typhoons regularly wreak havoc in the Philippines and China, not because of the sins of the people, but because it's a phenomena common to that region. For the same reason, we get hurricanes on the Gulf and the East Coast, and twisters from Texas to Kansas and beyond. Prevailing weather patterns bring rain to Seattle and hot, dry conditions to Death Valley.

Though it may seem that the weather is erratic, and we might get the idea that God personally decides every single time it should rain or not rain, He's generally no more involved in micromanaging the weather than He is with other natural phenomena. Weather patterns follow well-established natural laws. On the occasions when God intervenes in answer to prayer, He generally does so within the boundaries of established weather patterns. This is why people pray for rain and sometimes get rain. But you'd have to have phenomenal faith to pray for a week of rain in the Atacama Desert. And you're wasting your time if you pray for tropical temperatures at the South Pole in the middle of an Antarctic winter. God has established weather patterns, and He fully intends that they repeat themselves in annual cycles.

Longer weather cycles are also the cause of periodic extremes, storms, and shifting rainfall patterns. El Niño, which occurs every five years on average, alternately causes droughts or heavy rainfall (which in turn brings floods) in lands bordering the Pacific Ocean. Changes in ocean temperature cause fish stocks to migrate, directly affecting the fortunes of those who depend on fishing for their livelihood.

There are also longer weather cycles, such as the one that caused the Medieval Warm Period (950–1259), followed by a cooling-off known as the Little Ice Age (1350–1850). We appear to be heading into a new warm cycle right now—and whether this is aggravated by human activity or not is debatable.

One thing we know, however, is that it's not specific "acts of God" that cause most suffering, but mankind's own shortsightedness and selfishness. Genesis 2:15 (NIV) says, "The LORD God took the man and put him in the Garden of Eden to work it and take care of it." God intended for us to care for this world, but we're now reaping the results of centuries of *not* properly caring for it. "For they have sown the wind, and they shall reap the whirlwind" (Hosea 8:7 KJV).

For example, wanton deforestation and unwise agricultural methods cause erosion and desertification. Arid countries such as Spain, Greece, and Israel were once covered with forests and received more rainfall. Their climates changed when the forest cover disappeared. In addition, selfish industrialists pollute our soil, water, and air. They empty toxic waste into our streams, which makes its way into our water tables, lakes, and oceans. Rapid industrialization has left the air often unfit to breathe, and deforestation near the Gobi Desert in China has released tons of topsoil into the air as massive dust storms.

The increasing use of pesticides and fungicides on crops contribute to the Colony Collapse Disorder that is killing off honeybees by the millions—creating a threat to agriculture because honeybees pollinate more than thirty billion dollars' worth of crops in the US annually. The list of manmade disasters goes on and on.

When you consider all this, it's apparent that the bulk of our suffering as humans is self-inflicted. And our inherent selfishness is a result of our fallen nature. Since Adam and Eve's disobedience in the Garden of Eden, we've had the seeds of self-destruction within us. But as we've seen, many natural disasters *aren't* explained by mankind's activities.

Just the same, goodness prevails when God's children respond to disasters with compassion. Jesus says, " 'Truly I tell you, whatever you did for one of the least of these brothers and sisters of mine, you did for me' " (Matthew 25:40 NIV). When the early Christians heard that a severe famine was coming and would hit Judea hard, instead of sitting around speculating about its cause, or wondering who had sinned to cause it, they put their love into action. "The disciples, each according to his ability, determined to send relief to the brethren dwelling in Judea" (Acts 11:29 NKJV).

We're to be actively involved in feeding the hungry, clothing the poor, and giving financially to help disaster victims. Read Matthew 25:31–46 and you'll see what it means to be a follower of Jesus Christ. Read the story of the Good Samaritan in Luke 10:25–37 and you'll understand God's compassion for the world and His plan to relieve its suffering. It also shows that all people deserve our help, regardless of their race, culture, or religion. "If anyone has material possessions and sees a brother or sister in need but has no pity on them, how can the love of God be in that person? Dear children, let us not love with words or speech but with actions and in truth" (1 John 3:17–18 NIV).

This is why Christians, down through the ages until the present day, have been leaders in acts of mercy and compassion—they supply emergency food during famines, dig wells so impoverished communities can have clean drinking water, build orphanages and hospitals, care for lepers, and staff homeless shelters and soup kitchens. And Christian relief organizations supply emergency funds to help devastated regions rebuild after disasters.

God has great compassion and has set a plan in motion to tangibly meet the needs of the suffering. When you read the New Testament slowly and carefully, you get the clear message that God wants Christians—who have the Spirit of Jesus living in them—to be His boots on the ground, His hands of mercy to the suffering.

These are the *true* "acts of God."

5

Why Wars and Senseless Violence?

────────

The basis of all our relationships must be love. Jesus says, "'You shall love the LORD your God with all your heart, with all your soul, and with all your mind.' This is the first and great commandment. And the second is like it: 'You shall love your neighbor as yourself'" (Matthew 22:37–39 NKJV). Why is love so important? Some people think that loving others is a nice idea, if you can manage it; but their idea of love is little more than being polite, sort of like icing on a cake.

But we must truly *love* other human beings, regardless of race, ethnicity, nationality, or religion if we wish to avoid conflicts. If we love others, we'll respect them and avoid doing things to hurt them. "Love does no wrong to others" (Romans 13:10 NLT). But when we have prejudices and hatred, all kinds of suffering follow. This is tragic when it happens on a personal level. It's far worse when it happens on a national or international level.

The Bible asks: "From whence come wars and fightings among you? come they not hence, even of your lusts?" (James 4:1 KJV). *Lust* not only means coveting some another nation's oil, water, or land, but it can also refer to a bloodlust or a lust for vengeance—and wars, whether driven by greed, or by bigotry and ancient grievances, cause death, destruction, and suffering, not only for the combatants, but for civilians.

God tells the Israelites: "'See, I have set before you today life and good, death and evil, in that I command you today to love the LORD your God, to walk in His ways, and to keep His commandments'" (Deuteronomy 30:15–16 NKJV). These commands include: "'You shall love your neighbor as yourself'" (Leviticus 19:18 NKJV). God then concludes, "'I call heaven and earth as witnesses today against you, that I have set before you life and death, blessing and cursing; therefore choose life'" (Deuteronomy 30:19 NKJV).

Despite the fact that God gives us clear commands for life, man's inhumanity continues. And when it does, it's natural to ask, "Why doesn't God stop them?" But this in turn raises the question: "Stop *whom*? Only the greatest monsters—or *every* single person who wrongs someone else?" After all, the death of one person in an armed robbery is just as senseless and painful to his family as if he had died with a hundred others in a massacre. But if God were to nip all evil in the bud and prevent *all* injustice, oppression, and violence, He'd have to continually step in and execute judgment on every evildoer in the world—just before they acted. This is simply not going to happen.

God will one day sit in judgment upon every human being who has ever lived, and reward them or punish them for what they've done—but for the here and now He's gone into great detail in His Word explaining that *we* are to prevent crime, set up just laws to protect the vulnerable, restrain evildoers, and administer justice. He's left the implementing and the maintaining of a just society up to *us*. . .for now.

The Bible says, "A father of the fatherless, a defender of widows, is God in His holy habitation" (Psalm 68:5 NKJV). This verse can either comfort us greatly, or upset us greatly. After all, widows and orphans often suffer the most. Yet God looks out for the fatherless and widows. Over and over again in the Old Testament, and again in the New Testament, He states that it's imperative that His people care for the most vulnerable members of society—and warns that He will judge both society and individuals accordingly (Exodus 22:22–25; Deuteronomy 10:17–19; 14:28–29; 24:17–22; 27:19; Isaiah 1:17; Zechariah 7:10; Acts 6:1–6; 1 Timothy 5:3–4).

If you read the above references, you'll notice that God *also* includes strangers and resident foreigners among the vulnerable who are to receive protection and justice. A great deal of bigotry and conflict—not to mention pogroms and ethnic cleansings—would be eliminated if people would simply obey these commandments.

Yet, despite two World Wars, we haven't become more civilized and enlightened. We said, "Never again" after the systematic murder of nearly six million Jews by the Nazis, but the Holocaust was followed by several more atrocities—the slaughter of nearly two million peaceful Cambodians between 1976–1979 under Pol Pot; the ethnic cleansings perpetrated against Bosnians between 1992–1995; and the nearly one million Tutsis massacred by the Hutus in Rwanda in 1994.

Let's pause to address Hitler's attempt to exterminate the Jews, because some Christians believe that the Jewish people were cursed for all time for crucifying Jesus, and brought this horrific suffering on themselves. They draw this belief from Matthew 27:25 (NKJV) where a mob in Pilate's courtyard shouts, " 'His blood be on us, and on our children!' " But *not* all Jews were responsible for crucifying Jesus. Who then? The Bible says that "the chief priests, the scribes, and the elders of the people assembled at the palace of the high priest. . .and plotted to take Jesus by trickery and kill Him. But they said, 'Not during the feast, lest there be an uproar among the people' " (Matthew 26:3–5 NKJV).

"They wanted to arrest him, but they were afraid of the crowds" (Matthew 21:46 NLT). The common Jewish people loved Jesus and "heard him gladly" (Mark 12:37 KJV). They were the "great multitude" who cheered when He rode into Jerusalem (John 12:12). They would have rioted had the chief priests tried to arrest Jesus publicly. A multitude of such Jews became believers after Jesus rose from the dead (Acts 2:41; 4:4).

The Bible states that it was a small circle of

corrupt leaders—the chief priests, the scribes, and the elders—who plotted to kill Jesus (see Matthew 26:14, 47, 57, 59; 27:1–2; John 7:31–32). Jesus prophesied that He would die at their hands (Matthew 16:21). They sent a mob of zealous followers to arrest Jesus, and it was *that* mob that filled Pilate's courtyard and called down a curse upon themselves (Matthew 26:47; 27:20, 24–25).

The curse was not brought upon the heads of *all* Jews, *nor* for all time. It was fulfilled in Jesus' enemies and their (then-grown) children forty years later in AD 70 when Roman legions besieged Jerusalem and slew those who had been fighting against them. Yet the belief that all Jews were suffering for this curse was what helped Germans justify their extermination; this same skewed reasoning kept many Christians of other nations from being concerned about the plight of Jews in Nazi-occupied lands.

This same distorted logic allows some people today to explain away the slaughter of Cambodians, the deaths of Bosnians, and the massacre of Tutsis. If we allow ourselves to think that the victims must've done *something* to bring such calamity upon themselves, this defuses the troubling question of why they suffered, puts the blame at the doors of the victims themselves, and relieves us of the obligation to speak out on their behalf. But it does nothing to fulfill Christ's command to love our neighbors as ourselves.

This is why love is so crucial, and why it's foundational to Christ's teachings. War causes massive suffering. For example, between fifty million and eighty-five million people died in World War II, our greatest global conflict; millions more were wounded or maimed; millions suffered shell-shock or the trauma of losing loved ones; tens of millions went hungry or lost their homes.

In answer to the question above, "Stop *whom*?" many would answer, "Stop the greatest monsters first—the Hitlers and the Idi Amins and the Pol Pots. We'll work our way down the list later." So what would they have God do?

———

Scripture tells us that "the life of every living thing, and the breath of all mankind" (Job 12:10 NKJV) is in God's hand. This means that God could have ended Hitler's life had He chosen to. Or God could have *completely removed* Hitler's sanity and the Germans themselves would have locked him away—just as the Babylonian officials did to mad King Nebuchadnezzar. In fact, after Nebuchadnezzar's sanity was restored, he worshiped God, saying, "His dominion is an eternal dominion. . . . All the peoples of the earth are regarded as nothing. He does as he pleases with the powers of heaven and the peoples of the earth. No one can hold back his hand or say to him: 'What have you done?'" (Daniel 4:34–35 NIV).

So the question is: if God "does as he pleases with the peoples of the earth," and He *did* stop Nebuchadnezzar, why didn't He stop Hitler? Did He adopt a purely hands-off approach, despite the fact that He could have acted? If not, why did it take the Allies many long, grueling years of prayers and battles to defeat the Axis powers?

King David could have asked the same question. Despite the fact that he loved God passionately and pleased Him so much that God called him "'a man after My own heart'" (Acts 13:22 NKJV), after King Saul died, Saul's son didn't just hand the kingdom to David. Instead, "there was a long war between the house of Saul and the house of David" (2 Samuel 3:1 NKJV).

David had to fight hard, pray hard for victory, and learn perseverance.

Much of the answer boils down to the fact that God has given mankind freewill, and some people choose evil instead of good—and still others choose to do *great* evil and commit acts of violence on a massive scale. But God isn't going to intervene to forcibly put a stop to all wars and bring universal peace until the day that Christ returns and establishes His kingdom on earth. "He shall judge between many peoples, and rebuke strong nations afar off; and they shall beat their swords into plowshares, and their spears into pruning hooks: nation shall not lift up sword against nation, neither shall they learn war anymore" (Micah 4:3 NKJV).

Until that day, as Jesus said, " 'Nation will go to war against nation, and kingdom against kingdom' " (Matthew 24:7 NLT).

Some people have difficulty with the concept of fighting at all, even in self-defense, perhaps because the argument of "self-defense" has been abused so often. But although most wars are caused by selfish motives, there are righteous wars. And God has ordained a nation's military to protect its people from foreign aggressors, and police to deal with criminals and domestic terrorists (see Romans 13:1–5). Jesus says, " 'When a strong man, fully armed, guards his own palace, his goods are in peace' " (Luke 11:21 NKJV).

If you read the Bible carefully, you'll notice that God protected Israel in different ways. Sometimes He did the whole thing and didn't require their involvement. When they were about to be slaughtered by Pharaoh's army, God told them, " 'The Lord will fight for you; you need only to be still' " (Exodus 14:14 NIV). Most times, however, God helped Israel against her enemies. Before one battle He promised, " 'I will deliver all this great multitude into your hand' " (1 Kings 20:28 NKJV). God required their involvement, often with great effort and sacrifice, even at the cost of many lives.

In our day, the deaths of our men and women in uniform are not mere statistics. They're intensely personal for the families of those who die. But war is chaotic and claims many good lives. So what are we to think? Simply that " 'the sword devours one as well as another' " (2 Samuel 11:25 NIV), that "time and chance happen to them all" (Ecclesiastes 9:11 NKJV)?

But even if this were so, does that mean their

lives and their deaths lacked meaning? No, this is certainly not the case. Jesus says, " 'Greater love has no one than this, than to lay down one's life for his friends' " (John 15:13 NKJV). Their sacrifice was not in vain, and we must remember and honor them for it.

We are now involved in a War on Terror, a conflict of global proportions, and one that won't be settled easily or soon. For a previous generation, the attack on Pearl Harbor on December 7, 1941, was "a date which will live in infamy." The trumpet call for our generation was the destruction of the Twin Towers on September 11, 2001, when jihadists launched an attack on American soil and caused great loss of life.

When the dust settled, we realized that we'd been the target of a premeditated terrorist attack. We understood that we were at war. We knew that their objective was to cause terror and to strike a psychological blow, but because the issues were so clear-cut, it caused us to rise up and refuse to be cowed. It also brought us together as a nation and galvanized us into action. This isn't to say that we haven't made some miscalculations in response to perceived threats, but the point is this: Adversity strengthens our resolve. It can bring out the best and most heroic sides of us.

The Battle of Britain was a horrific ordeal for those who lived through it; London was repeatedly, mercilessly bombed while Spitfires and Hurricanes were locked with Messerschmitts in a life-or-death battle in the dark skies above. It was a terrible hour in Britain's history, a time of great suffering and fear and privation. Yet it is rightly remembered as their "finest hour." May we also rise to the occasion when duty calls.

———

Wars by foreign aggressors are one thing, but the senseless violence that frequently makes headlines is quite another. In recent years, we have repeatedly seen the face of evil—during the Oklahoma City bombing, the Aurora theater shootings, the cold-blooded massacre of innocent children at Newtown, and the indiscriminate murder and maiming of civilians during the Boston Marathon bombings. In each case, we were reminded of how the potential for great evil lurks in the human heart.

In the midst of the horror of these tragedies, however, selfless acts of heroism shone brightly. We will never forget the 343 firefighters who rushed up the steps of the burning Twin Towers to rescue others, and lost their lives as a result. And immediately following the Boston bombings, many people ran *toward* the explosions, oblivious to their personal safety, hoping to help. And who can forget the teacher's aide in Newtown who died attempting to shield a special-needs student in her arms—or the selfless people who threw their bodies between a loved one and the shooter in Aurora, Colorado?

And such tragedies also move millions of fellow citizens to compassion and generosity. When they hear about acts of senseless violence, many people's reaction is to do something to show that they care. Someone starts a fund for the survivors or their families, and the donations pour in. It does us good, when shocked by blatant evil, to be reminded that there's a great amount of good in this world as well. This can't make all the pain go away, but acts of Christian love and generosity go a long way toward answering questions we didn't even think to ask.

Good people doing acts of goodness can't bring back our lost loved ones, but when we desperately need to know that their lives counted for something, and to know that others are moved by our loss and share our grief, outpourings of empathy can be tremendously meaningful. And though we can't understand why God allowed it to happen, we know that He cares because *others* care. "Praise be to the. . .God of all comfort, who comforts us in all our troubles, so that we can comfort those in any trouble with the comfort we ourselves receive from God" (2 Corinthians 1:3–4 NIV).

Many people ascribe senseless violence to evolution, suggesting that it stems from humanity's origin as violent apes. They argue that such murderous behavior should not come as a surprise. For believers, however, there are serious questions. It's not that we blame God for what such perpetrators do. We recognize great evil when we see it. If anything, it vindicates the Bible's statement that there are moral absolutes—there is good and there definitely is evil. We also recognize that God's Word is right when it warns, "But know this, that in the last days perilous times will come: For men will be. . .without self-control, brutal, despisers of good" (2 Timothy 3:1–3 NKJV). "But evil men. . .will grow worse and worse" (2 Timothy 3:13 NKJV).

But the questions that remain are these:

"Why didn't God *prevent* these evil people from massacring the innocent? Why didn't He intervene instead of allowing psychotic killers to destroy others in such a senseless, cold-blooded manner?" And if you knew someone who was the victim of such an attack, the questions are: "Why was *my* loved one killed when the person right beside her was spared? Was my loved one not worthy? Or was God simply not *there* to protect her?"

You don't have to have lost a loved one in a mass shooting or a bombing to understand how deep the pain and how complex the questions can be. If you've been injured in a workplace accident, or lost a loved one in a traffic collision, you know what it is to suffer. While a traffic accident doesn't make international headlines like a terrorist attack or a school shooting, the physical, mental, and emotional trauma can be just as great.

Time and again, when we hear of fires at gas plants or explosions at fertilizer plants, speeding trains derailing, and buses going over escarpments, it's clear that *people* are at fault, whether through negligence or human error. God didn't cause this misery. In fact, God repeatedly acts to warn us, to bring details to our attention to *prevent* accidents and disasters. But though His acts of providence may far outnumber disasters, close calls don't make the headlines the way disasters do. And so our questions remain.

There are no easy answers, and because many responses depend on individual circumstances, we'd be foolish to attempt to give a one-size-fits-all answer. In fact, when someone is grieving the loss of a loved one, it's not particularly helpful to try to diagnose why God allowed the person to die. Chances are you'll give the wrong answer anyway.

At times like this, simply being there and sharing the survivors' sorrow is more important than attempting to give explanations. Job's friends made a mess of coming up with a reason for things. But they had the right attitude at first. When they heard about all he'd suffered, they went to visit him. The Bible tells us: "When they saw him. . .they began to weep aloud. . . . Then they sat on the ground with him for seven days and seven nights. No one said a word to him, because they saw how great his suffering was" (Job 2:12–13 NIV).

One of the dangers in seeking to explain

tragedy—beside the fact that it's *not* what the grieving person needs—is that we often give simplistic reasons such as, "Well, I guess God needed another angel in heaven." Nor is it helpful to make statements like, "Don't be sad. He's with God now." The grieving person has every right and need to be sad. So allow them to grieve. . . and grieve *with* them.

6

Why Financial and Relationship Problems?

Many Christians believe that if they pray, attend church, and tithe, God is obliged to pour out His blessings on them, give them material abundance, perfect health, and marital bliss—and keep them from accidents and all other misfortunes. Though the blessings in Deuteronomy 28:1–14 are covenant promises made specifically to the nation of Israel, many Christians believe these promises apply to us today as well.

In addition, the following passage explains why God's people suffered financial lack, and gave the solution: "'Will a man rob God? Yet you have robbed Me! But you say, "In what way have we robbed You?"' In tithes and offerings. You are cursed with a curse, for you have robbed Me, even this whole nation. Bring all the tithes into the storehouse, that there may be food in My house, and try Me now in this,'" says the LORD of hosts, "'If I will not open for you the windows of heaven and pour out for you such blessing that there will not be room enough to receive it. And I will rebuke the devourer for your sakes'" (Malachi 3:8–11 NKJV).

Those are powerful promises, and many Christians have given faithfully and have been blessed mightily in return—not entirely with material benefits, but often in other ways. They count themselves abundantly blessed already if God "rebukes the devourer" and keeps accidents, financial disasters, and sickness away. And of course, they're blessed spiritually because, as Jesus said, "'It is more blessed to give than to receive'" (Acts 20:35 NKJV).

Though Jesus had almost nothing to say about tithing, He did have a great deal to say about giving. Here is one such statement: "'Give, and you will receive. Your gift will return to you in full—pressed down, shaken together to make room for more, running over, and poured into your lap. The amount you give will determine the amount you get back'" (Luke 6:38 NLT). Although Jesus didn't specify that this would be in the form of finances, that's often what comes to mind. At any rate, it's reasonable to conclude that finances are *included*, since God has promised to supply all our needs (Philippians 4:19).

The truth is, millions of people have discovered to their joy that as they are faithful to pray for God's provision, reach out and help others, and give of their finances, God does indeed bless them. They might not always have overflowing abundance, but they have enough—and for this they are grateful. Yet, despite giving faithfully and sacrificially, hundreds of millions of other Christians have learned that this doesn't make them immune to financial struggles, unemployment, costly repair bills, sickness, family problems, and other setbacks.

How do we account for this, given the promises God has made? The first thing some churches advise is to look carefully at your giving to ensure you're paying "*all* the tithes" and are not actually shortchanging God. If that isn't the issue, they might suggest that you give *extra* offerings above and beyond your tithe. When you're desperate for a financial breakthrough, you're often advised to "give until it hurts"—even if you're *already* hurting.

Paul said, "He who sows sparingly will also reap sparingly, and he who sows bountifully will also reap bountifully." However, let's be honest: he wasn't describing a financial breakthrough plan, because the very next verse clarifies, "So let each one give as he purposes in his heart, not grudgingly or of necessity; for God loves a cheerful giver" (2 Corinthians 9:6–7 NKJV). While we *should* give generously, simply giving more and more is not God's blanket solution to all our financial and personal problems.

Sometimes we lack because God *is* withholding His blessings—though not for a lack of giving. The Bible says, "'Your iniquities have turned these things away, and your sins have withheld good from you'" (Jeremiah 5:25 NKJV). So in the event that something in our lives *is* out of line, we should ask God to point out the sin to us: "Search me, O God, and know my heart: try me, and know my thoughts: and see if there be any wicked way in me" (Psalm 139:23–24 KJV). We might be ignorant of our sins, but God isn't. "O God, you know how foolish I am; my sins cannot be hidden from you" (Psalm 69:5 NLT).

But we must also bear in mind that the surest sign of God's blessing isn't financial abundance— it's godly character. And hardships are often what it takes to build such character. This can be hard to grasp if our primary focus is to live the American Dream. There's nothing wrong with providing well for ourselves if we're able, as long as we don't lose sight of the fact that "'we must go through many hardships to enter the kingdom of God'" (Acts 14:22 NIV). This is a reality for millions of sincere Christians in China, India, and other nations, and it's increasingly becoming a reality in America as well.

Sometimes, in fact, Christians suffer precisely *because* they are Christians. Paul warned that "everyone who wants to live a godly life in Christ Jesus will suffer persecution" (2 Timothy 3:12 NLT). Believers in many countries are frequently ostracized for their faith and "share abundantly in the sufferings of Christ" (2 Corinthians 1:5 NIV). They're excluded from well-paying jobs, denied justice, and treated like third-class citizens. When it comes to material things, they feel blessed if they have a roof over their heads, enough food to eat, and clothing to wear.

Jesus says, "'I have come that they may have life, and that they may have it more abundantly'" (John 10:10 NKJV). If you read this verse in context, you'll see that He was referring specifically to eternal life and spiritual abundance. For years, however, many of us in the West have followed prosperity doctrines that declare that "abundant life" primarily means material affluence, perfect health, and all the desires of our hearts. Then we have a crisis of faith when we encounter setbacks and hardships.

Yet the apostle Paul writes: "I have learned to be content whatever the circumstances. I know what it is to be in need, and I know what it is to have plenty. I have learned the secret of being content in any and every situation, whether well fed or hungry, whether living in plenty or in want. . . . I have received full payment and have more than enough. I am amply supplied" (Philippians 4:11–12, 18 NIV).

Where was Paul when he declared that he had "more than enough"? He was under house arrest in Rome, living on an extremely tight budget. He wasn't going out on the town. We might think he was suffering, but Paul had a different perspective. Notice also that he writes, "I know what it is to be in need. . .hungry. . .in want." Many Christians might assume that Paul was somehow missing out on the abundant life. He wasn't.

Generally, getting a good education and working hard (and smart) ensures that we'll earn a good livelihood. But this isn't always the case.

"The race is not to the swift, nor the battle to the strong, nor bread to the wise, nor riches to men of understanding, nor favor to men of skill; but time and chance happen to them all" (Ecclesiastes 9:11 NKJV). This is especially true in developing nations where millions of Christians have limited opportunities to improve their lot, and where there are no government programs to soften the hard edges of reality. They can give faithfully, but still barely make it financially.

Many times, lack is not caused by sin, but by larger circumstances beyond our control. Say you're a fisherman in Peru, and every few years, like clockwork, El Niño prevents nutrient-rich cold waters from welling up, keeping away the mackerel and anchoveta. The result? Your livelihood suffers a downturn through no fault of your own. Or say you're a farmer in Ethiopia, and the entire region suffers an extended drought—as it did during the famine of 1983–85, and as it is right now in its eastern provinces. Again, you suffer, though not for anything you've done.

This principle also applies in the financial realm. Often we suffer because of overall economic conditions. Sometimes the selfish actions of individuals cause financial crises that put millions out of work. It's well-known that unscrupulous profiteers helped precipitate the recent economic recession. Solomon observed: "For man also does not know his time: like fish taken in a cruel net, like birds caught in a snare, so the sons of men are snared in an evil time, when it falls suddenly upon them" (Ecclesiastes 9:12 NKJV).

———

Paul said, "We are hard-pressed on every side, yet not crushed; we are perplexed, but not in despair" (2 Corinthians 4:8 NKJV). Being "hard-pressed on every side" can sometimes be a fact of life, along with being perplexed and uncertain. These can cause deep suffering. In fact, as doctors tell us, periods of prolonged stress are bad for both emotional and mental health—and even for physical health, because they can cause psychosomatic illnesses.

Years of financial pressures also put a strain on marriages. While statistics show that divorce rates actually went *down* during the recent recession (perhaps because people couldn't afford to break apart), the long-term attrition causes losses of retirement savings, bankruptcies, curtailing of leisure activities, end-of-month anxiety, and arguments. As Christians, we don't need to succumb to these pressures, but we're wise to acknowledge their existence.

Relationships between husbands and wives, parents and children, and between brothers and sisters, bring us not only our greatest joys and emotional security, but paradoxically, some of our greatest stress and grief. Many of us know what it's like to be betrayed or abandoned by someone we love—whether a husband, a wife, a family member, or a friend. This causes deep anguish. The emotional and mental pain can be excruciating.

In addition, many long-standing family feuds have begun over arguments about money— whether someone's out-of-control spending habits, a family loan that has gone unpaid, or quarrels over an inheritance. This results in anguish, arguments, and bitterness. Millions of people suffer day after day for this very reason. And though we don't necessarily blame it on God, the fact that it ruptures our relationship with other human beings is serious—as this affects our relationship with God.

The Bible says, " 'Do not seek revenge or bear

a grudge against anyone among your people, but love your neighbor as yourself. I am the LORD'" (Leviticus 19:18 NIV). When we bear a grudge against someone, or seek revenge, we're not loving the other person—and when we don't love him or her, we don't love God. This may sound like an overstatement, but it's true. "Whoever claims to love God yet hates a brother or sister is a liar. For whoever does not love their brother and sister, whom they have seen, cannot love God, whom they have not seen. And he has given us this command: Anyone who loves God must also love their brother and sister" (1 John 4:20–21 NIV).

The solution, difficult as it may be at times, is to love and to keep on loving, through thick and thin. "Love is patient, love is kind. . . . It does not dishonor others, it is not self-seeking, it is not easily angered, it keeps no record of wrongs" (1 Corinthians 13:4–5 NIV). How do we keep from nursing a grudge against someone? By keeping no record of wrongs, by continually forgiving. Jesus commands us to love even our *enemies* (Matthew 5:44), and this surely includes family members when they aggravate us, even if they break our hearts and bring unwanted stress into our lives.

———

Many Christians think that one of the primary benefits of suffering is that it causes us to be "broken," and that this is a good thing. If by this they mean that suffering causes us to be less dependent on ourselves and more dependent on God, to loosen our grasp on material things, and to be more compassionate toward others, then this is right. All too often, however, people seem to have the idea that being heartbroken, weeping, and at wit's end, is a desirable state. This is incorrect.

Jesus referred to Himself as the cornerstone of God's building, and said that " 'whoever falls on this stone will be broken; but on whomever it falls, it will grind him to powder' " (Matthew 21:44 NKJV). Some people believe that Jesus is giving us a choice: Either throw ourselves on Him and become mercifully "broken," or prepare for Him to fall on us in judgment. But Jesus was talking to His *enemies*, not advising believers how to respond to Him. He was telling His foes that no matter what they did to fight God, they couldn't win.

Jesus came to "heal the brokenhearted"

(Luke 4:18 KJV), not to *make* us brokenhearted and despairing. Yes, David said, "The LORD is close to the brokenhearted and saves those who are crushed in spirit" (Psalm 34:18 NIV). But He's near us because He's seen our state, has compassion on us and wants to resolve our troubles and comfort us—not because it's His goal to make us that way.

Consistently throughout the scriptures, being "broken" implies being shattered in judgment with no hope of being put back together (Jeremiah 19:1–2, 10–11). It also implies uselessness (Psalm 31:12) and weakness (Proverbs 15:13; 17:22). It makes little sense to say, "God wants to break you in pieces so that by gluing the broken pieces back together, He can make you a better vessel."

The Bible shows how God desires to make us into better vessels. If you read the story of Jeremiah at the potter's house (Jeremiah 18:1–11), you'll see that the potter found a flaw in the still-moist pot and by applying steady, firm pressure with his hands, pushed the yielding clay into a better shape. God then declared, "'Like clay in the hand of the potter, so are you in my hand, Israel'" (Jeremiah 18:6 NIV). Breaking and shattering is judgment on dry, brittle, hardened vessels that can no longer be changed. Pressure, molding, and reshaping are for vessels that are still moist and soft, still on the potter's wheel, still "a work in progress," and for whom there's hope of change.

The Hebrew words *lachats* and *muaqah* are translated as "affliction" in the King James Version the words literally mean "pressure." The Greek word *thlipsis*, which also means "pressure," is often translated as "affliction, anguish, tribulation and trouble." When God sends pressure on His children, it's usually the loving touch of the Master's hand, whose purpose is to change us for the better. This is often why God allows suffering.

Yes, there will be times when the circumstances that God allows to press our lives nearly cause us to approach the breaking point. As Paul writes, "We were under great pressure, far beyond our ability to endure, so that we despaired of life itself" (2 Corinthians 1:8 NIV). God allows circumstances in our lives that at times seem almost unbearable. Most of the time, however, our situation resembles this: "We are hard pressed on every side, but not crushed; perplexed, but not in despair" (2 Corinthians 4:8 NIV).

We are often under "great pressure" and "hard

pressed" because God is using that hard pressure to remold us. People are broken, however, when instead of softening their hearts in response to the pressure, they harden their hearts and resist it. The key is to yield, trust God, and soften our hearts in the process.

_____

Regarding financial suffering, many people state confidently that people on earth haven't even *begun* to suffer compared to how they will suffer in the near future. They see the present global recession as the precursor to total economic collapse, which will pave the way for a new financial world order, and the "mark of the beast" being forced on all the nations of the world.

Many zealous Christians are actually eager to see end-time events fulfilled, and they get excited when wars and economic crises happen. After all, according to one popular doctrine, Christians will be raptured from the earth just before the great tribulation begins. People who believe this see increasing global troubles and suffering as a positive thing—not for most of the world, to be sure, but for the church, at least.

Other Christians also closely follow

unfolding events, but warn that the church must go through the great tribulation and will only be raptured afterward. Following the rapture, the wrath of God will be poured out, culminating in the battle of Armageddon; then Jesus will set up His kingdom on earth. So they, too, look for things to get worse in the near future—not that any sane person would actually wish for suffering on a global scale, but because of the glorious dawn that follows this darkest of nights.

For some people, this renders the question of "why suffering?" almost irrelevant. After all, if the world will be destroyed in the next ten or so years, and then it's heaven on earth forever, there's no pressing need to ask why we suffer *now*—since all suffering will end imminently. Or so they hope. But as the decades drag on and things get worse, but not quite bad enough to bring the entire world crashing down, the questions regarding suffering remain in full force.

And this raises the question: What are we to do in the face of global problems so vast, so overwhelming, that we feel like a fleck of flotsam in a mighty, rushing river? Do we give up and say, "Well, I'll just enjoy life while I can. As long as my loved ones and I have enough, that's all that matters. Let us eat, drink, and be merry, for tomorrow we die!" (Luke 12:19; 1 Corinthians 15:32). No. This pessimistic view leads to complete selfishness and hedonism.

In contrast, Jesus tells us to live as overcomers despite the circumstances. He says, "'In this world you will have trouble. But take heart! I have overcome the world'" (John 16:33 NIV). Rather than drifting helplessly, or hunkering down in a cabin in the woods with a well, a supply of dry food, and ammunition, Jesus tells us, "Occupy till I come" (Luke 19:13 KJV). In other words, continue to live your faith daily, continue to love your children, continue to help your fellowman, continue to do what you can to alleviate pain and to comfort those who are suffering—until the very day that Jesus returns.

This much we can do, and this much God expects us to do, no matter what the state of the world, or the state of our personal finances. As Paul writes about the Christians of Macedonia, "They are being tested by many troubles, and they are very poor. But they are also filled with abundant joy, which has overflowed in rich generosity" (2 Corinthians 8:2 NLT).

7

Does God Truly Care?

━━━━━━━

Even though we know there's a God, we may have experienced so much pain and hardship that we might conclude that there's not necessarily any rhyme or reason to human misery. Any person, whether good or bad, is liable to endure suffering, and there's no real figuring it out. There's an element of truth to this, cynical as it might appear. The Bible tells us: "'People are born for trouble as readily as sparks fly up from a fire'" (Job 5:7 NLT). That's the way life is. We all get sick. We all feel pain. We all have accidents. Those who live long enough to grow old often suffer from failing health. And in the end we die.

Yes, we realize that our suffering gives us empathy for others who suffer; and yes, over the course of our lives we've experienced bad things that unexpectedly produced good results (Romans 8:28). Yet from a limited perspective, these bright spots may sometimes seem to get lost in a dark background of prolonged suffering. It's not that we wish to be cynical, but we resonate deeply with the statement: "There is something else meaningless that occurs on earth: the righteous who get what the wicked deserve, and the wicked who get what the righteous deserve" (Ecclesiastes 8:14 NIV).

We're well aware that, despite our best efforts to live righteously, we're not always blessed with prosperity, health, or acceptance. God *does* reward righteousness, and He *does* answer prayer, but not always according to our timetable, and not always the way we expect. And much of the time, frankly, it may seem as if He chooses not to answer at all.

We may feel like Job, whose friends tried to encourage him that if he'd just hang in there, just persevere, God would eventually bless him again. God would "'restore to you the years that the swarming locust has eaten'" (Joel 2:25 NKJV). But, like Job, some of us may have nearly given up hope that this will ever happen. When the locust has devoured so *many* years of our lives, and we're persuaded, like Naomi, that God Himself is intent on causing us grief, it's difficult to think that it will ever seem like a good idea to Him to bless us again.

Our experiences might have convinced

us that, although "God is love," it has to be a form of tough love that bears little resemblance to a normal definition of love. His dealings with mankind may seem not only inexplicable, but uncaring at times. We might even conclude that a God who allows thousands of people to die in an earthquake or an epidemic is exhibiting no sense of justice. As Job said in his most despondent moment, "'Innocent or wicked, it is all the same to God. That's why I say, He destroys both the blameless and the wicked.'" When a plague sweeps through, he laughs at the death of the innocent'" (Job 9:22–23 NLT).

God is certainly not laughing, but it can appear that He has sometimes left the room precisely when we needed Him most.

God usually can't be perceived by our physical senses. The Bible states, in fact, that He conceals Himself (Isaiah 45:15). Not only can we not see Him physically, but because He usually acts within the boundaries of natural physical laws, we normally don't see His actions directly either. Thus, when it seems that our prayers are going unanswered, it's easy to ask, "Why do You stand afar off, O LORD? Why do You hide in times of trouble?" (Psalm 10:1 NKJV). When we desperately need God's help, He doesn't respond. This not only baffles us, but can add to our overall feeling that life just doesn't make sense.

Much suffering in life seems to be senseless, and if this life is the entire scope of reality, then many things truly *are* senseless. Consider the injustice of the following story if this world is all that there is, and death is the end. You've read it before, but read it again: "'There was a certain rich man who was splendidly clothed in purple and fine linen and who lived each day in luxury. At his gate lay a poor man named Lazarus who was covered with sores. As Lazarus lay there longing for scraps from the rich man's table, the dogs would come and lick his open sores. Finally, the poor man died. . . . The rich man also died'" (Luke 16:19–22 NLT).

What if *that's* where the story ended? One man lives with great wealth, perfect health, and no troubles, yet right next to him, another man lives in abject poverty, in constant hunger, with daily sickness, and no relief from his misery. Then they both die. The end. What could we possibly be left to conclude about the love and justice of God?

The apostle Paul glumly admits, "If in this

life only we have hope in Christ, we are of all men most miserable" (1 Corinthians 15:19 KJV).

But the story *doesn't* end there. And the death of our physical bodies isn't the end of our existence. Jesus went on to say that Lazarus " 'was carried by the angels to be with Abraham' " (Luke 16:22 NLT). As Abraham explained to the former rich man, " 'Son, remember that during your lifetime you had everything you wanted, and Lazarus had nothing. So now he is here being comforted' " (Luke 16:25 NLT).

The book of Revelation explains how people like Lazarus are comforted in the world to come: " 'Therefore they are before the throne of God, and serve Him day and night in His temple. And He who sits on the throne will dwell among them. They shall neither hunger anymore nor thirst anymore; the sun shall not strike them, nor any heat; for the Lamb who is in the midst of the throne will shepherd them and lead them to living fountains of waters' " (Revelation 7:15–17 NKJV).

Jesus says, " 'In My Father's house are many mansions; if it were not so, I would have told you. I go to prepare a place for you' " (John 14:2 NKJV). And Paul reminds us, " 'No eye has seen, no ear has heard, and no mind has imagined what God has prepared for those who love him'" (1 Corinthians 2:9 NLT). "Therefore we do not lose heart. Though outwardly we are wasting away, yet inwardly we are being renewed day by day. For our light and momentary troubles are achieving for us an eternal glory that far outweighs them all. So we fix our eyes not on what is seen, but on what is unseen, since what is seen is temporary, but what is unseen is eternal" (2 Corinthians 4:16–18 NIV).

Abraham, the father of our faith, asked, "'Shall not the Judge of all the earth do right?'" (Genesis 18:25 NKJV). And indeed God *will* do what is right. "'God will wipe away every tear from their eyes; there shall be no more death, nor sorrow, nor crying. There shall be no more pain. . . .' Then He who sat on the throne said, 'Behold, I make all things new'" (Revelation 21:4–5 NKJV). Our brief life on earth may be filled with sorrow and injustice, but this world we live in is only temporary, whereas the world that awaits—though presently unseen—will last forever.

The promise of eternal life and never-ending joy seems almost too good to be true. How can we be sure that such a paradise actually exists? Because Jesus said, "'If it were not so, I would have told you'" (John 14:2 NKJV).

So how do we get there? Jesus added, "'I am the way and the truth and the life. No one comes to the Father except through me'" (John 14:6 NIV). "'For God so loved the world that he gave his one and only Son, that whoever believes in him shall not perish but have eternal life'" (John 3:16 NIV). God sent His Son to earth to become a man, to experience all the pain and sorrow that we experience, and to die on the cross for our sins. Jesus knows what we go through. "We do not have a High Priest who cannot sympathize with our weaknesses, but was in all points tempted as we are" (Hebrews 4:15 NKJV).

Yet, despite the fact that Jesus had great compassion on His people and did nothing but good, they rejected Him. "He came into the very world he created, but the world didn't recognize him. He came to his own people, and even they rejected him" (John 1:10–11 NLT). Isaiah prophesied, "He is despised and rejected of men; a Man of sorrows and acquainted with grief. And we hid. . .our faces from Him" (Isaiah 53:3 NKJV).

Job, Naomi, and Lazarus all suffered—

seemingly senselessly—but Jesus was the ultimate example of a righteous man who was rejected, falsely accused, and suffered the shameful death of a common criminal, experiencing intense physical and psychological pain in the process. And the cross was just *part* of His suffering. The Gospels only briefly mention the flogging He endured, saying, "Then Pilate took Jesus and had him flogged" (John 19:1 NIV), yet this was a brutal torture.

Flogging was no token punishment. A person frequently didn't survive it, and Roman authors referred to it as "the half death." The Jews limited a scourging to "forty lashes minus one" (2 Corinthians 11:24 NIV), but the Romans had no such limits. It was up to the soldiers how many lashes someone received, and the soldiers who beat Jesus were Thracians of the Tenth Legion, renowned for their cruelty.

Jesus was first stripped naked and His hands were bound to a whipping post. Then two Roman soldiers, called *lictors*, one standing behind to the left, the other to the right, alternated in whipping. Forceful blows were delivered to His shoulders, His back, His buttocks, and His upper legs—all the way down to His feet.

The Roman scourge was called a *flagellum*, and consisted of a wooden handle with leather thongs; several iron or lead balls and pieces of sheep bone were attached to each strip of leather. At first, these objects caused the blood vessels below the skin to break. Then the blows cut through the skin and underlying tissues. As the beating continued, they lacerated the muscles. Jesus' back was soon cut open in stripes. Not only was the pain intense, but His body was so savagely whipped that multiple arteries were ripped open. Blood loss was dramatic, and Jesus' body went into hypovolemic shock, leaving Him so weak that He was unable to carry His cross to the place of crucifixion (Luke 23:26).

Crucifixion was the ultimate instrument of torture and death. Its goal was not merely to kill its victims, but to bring about death in the most painful way possible. Iron nails were driven between Christ's two wrist bones, severing the median nerve as they pinned His hands to the crossbeam. The pain was excruciating. After that, a nail was driven through His feet.

Jesus could inhale while hanging in a slumped position, but to exhale He had to raise himself up. However, to raise Himself up, He had to push up against the nail in His feet and pull against the nails through His wrists, causing unbelievable pain. This torment was so intense that the word, "excruciating" (Latin *ex-cruciare*, "from the cross"), was invented to describe it. Not only did Jesus suffer severe muscle cramps, but His back, laid wide open by scourging, constantly scraped against the rough wood of the cross, as He repeatedly pulled Himself up, then slumped down. Jesus was wracked with torment at every moment.

When Jesus was nailed to the cross, "they gave him vinegar to drink mingled with gall" (Matthew 27:34 KJV). The following prophecy shows what He experienced at this time: "Reproach has broken my heart, and I am full of heaviness; I looked for someone to take pity, but there was none; and for comforters, but I found none. They also gave me gall for my food, and for my thirst they gave me vinegar to drink" (Psalm 69:20–21 NKJV).

Job had felt utterly condemned and abandoned by God. So did Jesus. With His final breath He called out, " 'My God, My God, why have You forsaken Me?' " (Matthew 27:46 NKJV). He didn't shout this for dramatic effect. Jesus actually felt that His Father had abandoned Him. Being rejected by His people was bad enough. But feeling rejected by God was agonizing. In eternity past, Jesus had dwelled "in the bosom of the Father" (John 1:18 NKJV), and being cut off from Him was more than He could bear. Jesus died literally of a broken heart.

Dramatic blood loss and asphyxiation resulting from exhaustion were probably the chief causes of His death. But the fact that "Jesus cried out with a loud voice, and breathed His last" (Mark 15:37 NKJV) suggests that He may have suffered a sudden cardiac rupture caused by a dislodged blood clot, induced by the severe physical and emotional trauma. Yes, Jesus suffered intense emotional trauma.

In a world full of senseless pain and suffering, where the wicked prosper and the righteous are tormented—while God seems to be standing back and doing nothing—this was the ultimate senseless injustice. This was a chilling fulfillment of Solomon's lament: "There is something else meaningless that occurs on earth: the righteous who get what the wicked deserve, and the wicked who get what the righteous deserve" (Ecclesiastes 8:14 NIV).

But this story has the happiest of all possible endings, and Jesus' death was infused with powerful meaning. After lying in a tomb for three days, He was raised from the dead with great power to live and to reign forever at the right hand of God. And by His suffering and His dying, He paid the price for all of our sins, and made a way for us also to live on after the death of our physical bodies, and to enter the presence of God. Jesus' shameful, agonizing death on the cross made it possible for all wrongs in our lives to be righted, all injustices to be corrected, and all pain and suffering to be compensated.

By His crucifixion and His following glorious resurrection, Jesus brought ultimate good and meaning to a world filled with pain and suffering. And there is more wonderful news for us. Jesus says, "'Because I live, you will live also'" (John 14:19 NKJV).

———

In the previous chapter, I cautioned against the overzealous desire of some Christians for end-time cataclysms to overwhelm the earth. Yet, the truth is, whether these traumatic events happen within our lifetime or not, the world *is* eventually going to end, and Jesus *will* reign over the nations. Heaven will come down to the earth, and God will personally dwell among us.

Not only will God live among us, but we shall once again be united with our departed loved ones, whose loss left such a void in our hearts. And we'll be with them in an everlasting Paradise. This bright hope has sustained many a believer down through the ages, when the burdens of this life have seemed to be almost too much to bear. In that day, all wrongs will be righted, all our tears will be dried, and all of our painful questions will be answered.

One day soon " 'the kingdoms of this world [will] become the kingdoms of our Lord and of His Christ, and He shall reign forever and ever!' " (Revelation 11:15 NKJV). "He who testifies to these things says, 'Surely I am coming quickly.' Amen. Even so, come, Lord Jesus!" (Revelation 22:20 NKJV).

In the meantime, we still suffer. "We always carry around in our body the death of Jesus, so that the life of Jesus may also be revealed in our body" (2 Corinthians 4:10 NIV). Paul said that he welcomed suffering for Jesus' sake, because he wanted to "know Him and the power of His resurrection, and the fellowship of His sufferings" (Philippians 3:10 NKJV). But the good news is this: "If we suffer, we shall also reign with him" (2 Timothy 2:12 KJV).

Much of our suffering, however, seems to be simply a part of the human condition, random and unrelated to suffering for Jesus. But God sees *all* of our pain. And though it's true that He doesn't intervene to prevent every accident, sickness, or disaster, He loves us and cares immensely. God said of the suffering of the Hebrews in Egypt, "'I know their sorrows'" (Exodus 3:7 NKJV). He knows every bit of our suffering, and every tear that we shed. This is one reason that Jesus was called "a man of sorrows, and acquainted with grief" (Isaiah 53:3 KJV).

He not only knows when we experience grief, but He personally feels our pain. "In all their suffering he also suffered" (Isaiah 63:9 NLT).

God doesn't cause evil, but in His great love for us, He constantly redeems evil situations and events. God is good. He is loving. As David said, "You are good, and do good" (Psalm 119:68 NKJV).

Appendix A

Deuteronomy 28
(New International Version)

Blessings for Obedience

¹ If you fully obey the LORD your God and carefully follow all his commands I give you today, the LORD your God will set you high above all the nations on earth. ² All these blessings will come on you and accompany you if you obey the LORD your God:

³ You will be blessed in the city and blessed in the country.

⁴ The fruit of your womb will be blessed, and the crops of your land and the young of your livestock—the calves of your herds and the lambs of your flocks.

⁵ Your basket and your kneading trough will be blessed.

⁶ You will be blessed when you come in and blessed when you go out.

⁷ The LORD will grant that the enemies who rise up against you will be defeated before you. They will come at you from one direction but flee from you in seven.

⁸ The LORD will send a blessing on your barns and on everything you put your hand to. The

Lord your God will bless you in the land he is giving you.

⁹ The Lord will establish you as his holy people, as he promised you on oath, if you keep the commands of the Lord your God and walk in obedience to him. ¹⁰ Then all the peoples on earth will see that you are called by the name of the Lord, and they will fear you. ¹¹ The Lord will grant you abundant prosperity—in the fruit of your womb, the young of your livestock and the crops of your ground—in the land he swore to your ancestors to give you.

¹² The Lord will open the heavens, the storehouse of his bounty, to send rain on your land in season and to bless all the work of your hands. You will lend to many nations but will borrow from none. ¹³ The Lord will make you the head, not the tail. If you pay attention to the commands of the Lord your God that I give you this day and carefully follow them, you will always be at the top, never at the bottom. ¹⁴ Do not turn aside from any of the commands I give you today, to the right or to the left, following other gods and serving them.

Curses for Disobedience

[15] However, if you do not obey the LORD your God and do not carefully follow all his commands and decrees I am giving you today, all these curses will come on you and overtake you:

[16] You will be cursed in the city and cursed in the country.

[17] Your basket and your kneading trough will be cursed.

[18] The fruit of your womb will be cursed, and the crops of your land, and the calves of your herds and the lambs of your flocks.

[19] You will be cursed when you come in and cursed when you go out.

[20] The LORD will send on you curses, confusion and rebuke in everything you put your hand to, until you are destroyed and come to sudden ruin because of the evil you have done in forsaking him. [21] The LORD will plague you with diseases until he has destroyed you from the land you are entering to possess. [22] The LORD will strike you with wasting disease, with fever and inflammation, with scorching heat and drought, with blight and mildew, which will plague you until you perish. [23] The sky over your head will be bronze, the ground beneath

you iron. [24] The LORD will turn the rain of your country into dust and powder; it will come down from the skies until you are destroyed.

[25] The LORD will cause you to be defeated before your enemies. You will come at them from one direction but flee from them in seven, and you will become a thing of horror to all the kingdoms on earth. [26] Your carcasses will be food for all the birds and the wild animals, and there will be no one to frighten them away. [27] The LORD will afflict you with the boils of Egypt and with tumors, festering sores and the itch, from which you cannot be cured. [28] The LORD will afflict you with madness, blindness and confusion of mind. [29] At midday you will grope about like a blind person in the dark. You will be unsuccessful in everything you do; day after day you will be oppressed and robbed, with no one to rescue you.

[30] You will be pledged to be married to a woman, but another will take her and rape her. You will build a house, but you will not live in it. You will plant a vineyard, but you will not even begin to enjoy its fruit. [31] Your ox will be slaughtered before your eyes, but you will eat none of it. Your donkey will be forcibly taken from you and will not be returned. Your sheep

will be given to your enemies, and no one will rescue them. ³² Your sons and daughters will be given to another nation, and you will wear out your eyes watching for them day after day, powerless to lift a hand. ³³ A people that you do not know will eat what your land and labor produce, and you will have nothing but cruel oppression all your days. ³⁴ The sights you see will drive you mad. ³⁵ The LORD will afflict your knees and legs with painful boils that cannot be cured, spreading from the soles of your feet to the top of your head.

³⁶ The LORD will drive you and the king you set over you to a nation unknown to you or your ancestors. There you will worship other gods, gods of wood and stone. ³⁷ You will become a thing of horror, a byword and an object of ridicule among all the peoples where the LORD will drive you.

³⁸ You will sow much seed in the field but you will harvest little, because locusts will devour it. ³⁹ You will plant vineyards and cultivate them but you will not drink the wine or gather the grapes, because worms will eat them. ⁴⁰ You will have olive trees throughout your country but you will not use the oil, because the olives will drop off. ⁴¹ You will have sons and daughters but

you will not keep them, because they will go into captivity. [42] Swarms of locusts will take over all your trees and the crops of your land.

[43] The foreigners who reside among you will rise above you higher and higher, but you will sink lower and lower. [44] They will lend to you, but you will not lend to them. They will be the head, but you will be the tail.

[45] All these curses will come on you. They will pursue you and overtake you until you are destroyed, because you did not obey the LORD your God and observe the commands and decrees he gave you. [46] They will be a sign and a wonder to you and your descendants forever. [47] Because you did not serve the LORD your God joyfully and gladly in the time of prosperity, [48] therefore in hunger and thirst, in nakedness and dire poverty, you will serve the enemies the LORD sends against you. He will put an iron yoke on your neck until he has destroyed you.

[49] The LORD will bring a nation against you from far away, from the ends of the earth, like an eagle swooping down, a nation whose language you will not understand, [50] a fierce-looking nation without respect for the old or pity for the young. [51] They will devour the

young of your livestock and the crops of your land until you are destroyed. They will leave you no grain, new wine or olive oil, nor any calves of your herds or lambs of your flocks until you are ruined. [52] They will lay siege to all the cities throughout your land until the high fortified walls in which you trust fall down. They will besiege all the cities throughout the land the LORD your God is giving you.

[53] Because of the suffering your enemy will inflict on you during the siege, you will eat the fruit of the womb, the flesh of the sons and daughters the LORD your God has given you. [54] Even the most gentle and sensitive man among you will have no compassion on his own brother or the wife he loves or his surviving children, [55] and he will not give to one of them any of the flesh of his children that he is eating. It will be all he has left because of the suffering your enemy will inflict on you during the siege of all your cities. [56] The most gentle and sensitive woman among you— so sensitive and gentle that she would not venture to touch the ground with the sole of her foot— will begrudge the husband she loves and her own son or daughter [57] the afterbirth from her womb and the children she bears. For in her dire need

she intends to eat them secretly because of the suffering your enemy will inflict on you during the siege of your cities.

⁵⁸ If you do not carefully follow all the words of this law, which are written in this book, and do not revere this glorious and awesome name— the LORD your God— ⁵⁹ the LORD will send fearful plagues on you and your descendants, harsh and prolonged disasters, and severe and lingering illnesses. ⁶⁰ He will bring on you all the diseases of Egypt that you dreaded, and they will cling to you. ⁶¹ The LORD will also bring on you every kind of sickness and disaster not recorded in this Book of the Law, until you are destroyed. ⁶² You who were as numerous as the stars in the sky will be left but few in number, because you did not obey the LORD your God. ⁶³ Just as it pleased the LORD to make you prosper and increase in number, so it will please him to ruin and destroy you. You will be uprooted from the land you are entering to possess.

⁶⁴ Then the LORD will scatter you among all nations, from one end of the earth to the other. There you will worship other gods—gods of wood and stone, which neither you nor your

ancestors have known. [65] Among those nations you will find no repose, no resting place for the sole of your foot. There the LORD will give you an anxious mind, eyes weary with longing, and a despairing heart. [66] You will live in constant suspense, filled with dread both night and day, never sure of your life. [67] In the morning you will say, "If only it were evening!" and in the evening, "If only it were morning!"—because of the terror that will fill your hearts and the sights that your eyes will see. [68] The LORD will send you back in ships to Egypt on a journey I said you should never make again. There you will offer yourselves for sale to your enemies as male and female slaves, but no one will buy you.

Appendix B

Selected Bible Promises
Faithfulness, God's

*Know therefore that the LORD thy God, he is God,
the faithful God, which keepeth covenant and mercy
with them that love him and keep his commandments
to a thousand generations.*

DEUTERONOMY 7:9

*(For the LORD thy God is a merciful God;) he will
not forsake thee, neither destroy thee, nor forget the
covenant of thy fathers which he sware unto them.*

DEUTERONOMY 4:31

*He hath remembered his covenant for ever, the word
which he commanded to a thousand generations.*

PSALM 105:8

*God is not a man, that he should lie; neither the son
of man, that he should repent: hath he said, and
shall he not do it? or hath he spoken, and shall he
not make it good?*

NUMBERS 23:19

*Let us hold fast the profession of our faith without
wavering; (for he is faithful that promised).*

HEBREWS 10:23

If we believe not, yet he abideth faithful: he cannot deny himself.

2 TIMOTHY 2:13

The Lord is not slack concerning his promise, as some men count slackness; but is longsuffering to us—ward.

2 PETER 3:9

Blessed be the LORD, that hath given rest unto his people Israel, according to all that he promised: there hath not failed one word of all his good promise.

1 KINGS 8:56

O Lord, thou art my God; I will exalt thee, I will praise thy name; for thou hast done wonderful things; thy counsels of old are faithfulness and truth.

ISAIAH 25:1

And they that know thy name will put their trust in thee: for thou, LORD, hast not forsaken them that seek thee.

PSALM 9:10

Thy word is true from the beginning: and every one of thy righteous judgments endureth for ever.

PSALM 119:160

For ever, O LORD, thy word is settled in heaven. Thy faithfulness is unto all generations.

PSALM 119:89–90

And also the Strength of Israel will not lie nor repent: for he is not a man, that he should repent.

1 SAMUEL 15:29

For all the promises of God in him are yea, and in him Amen, unto the glory of God by us.

2 CORINTHIANS 1:20

My covenant will I not break, nor alter the thing that is gone out of my lips.

PSALM 89:34

For the mountains shall depart, and the hills be removed; but my kindness shall not depart from thee, neither shall the covenant of my peace be removed, saith the LORD that hath mercy on thee.

ISAIAH 54:10

Yea, I have spoken it, I will also bring it to pass; I have purposed it, I will also do it.

ISAIAH 46:11

Love, God's

For God so loved the world, that he gave his only begotten Son, that whosoever believeth in him should not perish, but have everlasting life.

JOHN 3:16

And he will love thee, and bless thee, and multiply thee: he will also bless the fruit of thy womb, and the fruit of thy land, thy corn, and thy wine, and thine oil, the increase of thy kine, and the flocks of thy sheep, in the land which he sware unto thy fathers to give thee.

DEUTERONOMY 7:13

The LORD openeth the eyes of the blind: the LORD raiseth them that are bowed down: the LORD loveth the righteous.

PSALM 146:8

The way of the wicked is an abomination unto the LORD: but he loveth him that followeth after righteousness.

PROVERBS 15:9

For as a young man marrieth a virgin, so shall thy sons marry thee: and as the bridegroom rejoiceth over the bride, so shall thy God rejoice over thee.

ISAIAH 62:5

The LORD thy God in the midst of thee is mighty; he will save, he will rejoice over thee with joy; he will rest in his love, he will joy over thee with singing.

ZEPHANIAH 3:17

The LORD hath appeared of old unto me, saying, Yea, I have loved thee with an everlasting love: therefore with lovingkindness have I drawn thee.

JEREMIAH 31:3

I will heal their backsliding, I will love them freely: for mine anger is turned away from him.

HOSEA 14:4

Yea, I will rejoice over them to do them good, and I will plant them in this land assuredly with my whole heart and with my whole soul.

JEREMIAH 32:41

But God, who is rich in mercy, for his great love wherewith he loved us, even when we were dead in sins, hath quickened us together with Christ, (by grace ye are saved;) and hath raised us up together, and made us sit together in heavenly places in Christ Jesus: That in the ages to come he might shew the exceeding riches of his grace in his kindness toward us through Christ Jesus.

EPHESIANS 2:4–7

Herein is love, not that we loved God, but that he loved us, and sent his Son to be the propitiation for our sins.

1 John 4:10

And we have known and believed the love that God hath to us. God is love; and he that dwelleth in love dwelleth in God, and God in him.

1 John 4:16

We love him, because he first loved us.

1 John 4:19

And I have declared unto them thy name, and will declare it: that the love wherewith thou hast loved me may be in them, and I in them.

John 17:26

I in them, and thou in me, that they may be made perfect in one; and that the world may know that thou hast sent me, and hast loved them, as thou hast loved me.

John 17:23

For the Father himself loveth you, because ye have loved me, and have believed that I came out from God.

John 16:27

Now our Lord Jesus Christ himself, and God, even our Father, which hath loved us, and hath given us everlasting consolation and good hope through grace, comfort your hearts, and stablish you in every good word and work.

2 THESSALONIANS 2:16–17

Protection, God's

The name of the LORD is a strong tower: the righteous runneth into it, and is safe.

PROVERBS 18:10

The angel of the LORD encampeth round about them that fear him, and delivereth them.

PSALM 34:7

For the eyes of the Lord run to and fro throughout the whole earth, to shew himself strong in the behalf of them whose heart is perfect toward him. Herein thou hast done foolishly: therefore from henceforth thou shalt have wars.

2 CHRONICLES 16:9

The Lord shall preserve thee from all evil: he shall preserve thy soul. The Lord shall preserve thy going out and thy coming in from this time forth, and even for evermore.

Psalm 121:7–8

When thou liest down, thou shalt not be afraid: yea, thou shalt lie down, and thy sleep shall be sweet.

Proverbs 3:24

And who is he that will harm you, if ye be followers of that which is good?

1 Peter 3:13

The beloved of the Lord shall dwell in safety by him; and the Lord shall cover him all the day long, and he shall dwell between his shoulders.

Deuteronomy 33:12

He shall not be afraid of evil tidings: his heart is fixed, trusting in the Lord.

Psalm 112:7

But whoso hearkeneth unto me shall dwell safely, and shall be quiet from fear of evil.

Proverbs 1:33

Because thou hast made the LORD, which is my refuge, even the most High, thy habitation; there shall no evil befall thee, neither shall any plague come nigh thy dwelling.

PSALM 91:9–10

But now thus saith the LORD that created thee, O Jacob, and he that formed thee, O Israel, Fear not: for I have redeemed thee, I have called thee by thy name; thou art mine. When thou passest through the waters, I will be with thee; and through the rivers, they shall not overflow thee: when thou walkest through the fire, thou shalt not be burned; neither shall the flame kindle upon thee.

ISAIAH 43:1–2

And they shall no more be a prey to the heathen, neither shall the beast of the land devour them; but they shall dwell safely, and none shall make them afraid.

EZEKIEL 34:28

I will both lay me down in peace, and sleep: for thou, LORD, only makest me dwell in safety.

PSALM 4:8

The Lord is my light and my salvation; whom shall I fear? the Lord is the strength of my life; of whom shall I be afraid?

Psalm 27:1

Scripture Index

Revelation